THE ULTIMATE BOOK OF

USELESS
INFORMATION

THE ULTIMATE BOOK OF
USELESS
INFORMATION

A Few Thousand More Things You Might Need to Know
(But Probably Don't)

NOEL BOTHAM
AND THE USELESS INFORMATION SOCIETY

A PERIGEE BOOK

tarcherperigee

An imprint of Penguin Random House LLC
375 Hudson Street
New York, New York 10014
penguin.com

First published by Perigee, an imprint of
Penguin Group (USA) Inc. 2006
This volume first published 2018

Jacket art by Getty Images
Jacket design by Ben Gibson
Text design by Tiffany Estreicher

Special Markets ISBN: 978-1-101-94864-4

Printed in the United States of America
3 5 7 9 10 8 6 4

Members of The Useless Information Society

CONTENTS

THERE'S NO BUSINESS LIKE...

ALSO KNOWN AS

Dean Martin, born Dino Crocetti, boxed under the name Kid Crochet as a teenager.

The film version of *Oliver Twist* had its name changed to *Lost Child in Foggy City* when it was shown in China.

Tennessee Williams's real name was Thomas Lanier Williams.

The Marx Brothers started their show-business career as the Six Mascots, featuring brothers Leonard; Adolph; Julius; Milton; their mother, Minnie; and their aunt Hannah. Later the brothers changed their names to Chico, Harpo, Groucho, and Gummo, respectively.

Samuel Goldwyn's real name was Samuel Goldfish.

Before he became a comedian Bob Hope was a boxer known as Packy East.

The first name of TV detective Lieutenant Columbo was Phillip.

W. C. Fields's full name was William Claude Dukenfield.

In *Arsenic and Old Lace* starring Cary Grant, a tombstone shown in the film is inscribed with Grant's real name, Archibald Leach.

When Katherine Hepburn was a child she shaved her head, wore trousers, and called herself "Jimmy" because she so wanted to be a boy.

Boris Karloff's real name was William Henry Pratt, and he was educated at Dulwich College, England.

Richard Gere's middle name is Tiffany.

Simon Templar was dubbed "the Saint" because of his initials "S.T."

When Bugs Bunny made his first appearance in 1935 he was called Happy Rabbit.

The *Flintstones* lawyer who never lost a case was called Perry Masonry.

The original title of the television series *Charlie's Angels* was *The Alley Cats*.

Leonard Skinner was the name of the gym teacher of the boys who went on to form Lynyrd Skynyrd. He once told them: "You boys will never amount to nothing" The band's front man, Ronnie Van Zant, decided to adopt the name but change the spelling, as a joke on his former teacher.

When Tom and Jerry made their debut in the 1940 cartoon *Puss Gets the Boot*, Tom was called Jasper and Jerry didn't have a name at all.

The captain of the USS *Enterprise* in *Star Trek*, before James T. Kirk ever came on board, was Captain Christopher Pike. In the original draft for *Star Trek*, the name of the USS *Enterprise* was the USS *Yorktowne*.

The full name of the Fonz, played by Henry Winkler in the TV series *Happy Days*, was Arthur Herbert Fonzarelli.

Singer Bob Dylan appeared in the 1973 film *Pat Garrett & Billy the Kid* as the character Alias. Dylan's real name is Robert Zimmerman.

Indiana Jones's first name was Henry.

Rita Hayworth's real name was Margarita Cansino.

Woody Allen's legal name is Heywood Allen, but his real name was originally Allen Stewart Konigsberg.

Arnold Schwarzenegger made his screen debut as Arnold Strong in the 1970 Italian TV film *Hercules in New York*.

The roaring lion in the MGM logo was named Volney and lived at the Memphis Zoo.

John Wayne began his film career in a series of Westerns as Singin' Sam, the silver screen's first singing cowboy. Unfortunately, he couldn't make records because his singing voice and guitar playing were both dubbed.

Elton John's real name is Reginald Dwight. "Elton" came from Elton Dean, a Bluesology sax player, and "John" came from Long John Baldry, founder of Blues Inc.

Hulk Hogan's real name is Terry Bolle.

Colonel Sherman Potter's horse in the TV series *M*A*S*H* was named Sophie.

Bert's goldfish in the TV series *Sesame Street* were named Lyle and Talbot, after the actor Lyle Talbot.

Ian Anderson, not Jethro Tull, is the name of the rock singer responsible for such songs as "Aqualung" and "Thick as a Brick." Jethro Tull is the name of the band. And the original Jethro Tull was an English horticulturist who invented the seed drill.

ALMOST KNOWN AS . . .

Oprah Winfrey's first name should have been the biblical name Orpah, from the Book of Ruth, except the midwife made a mistake in spelling it when she filled out the birth certificate.

MISSED OPPORTUNITIES

Despite being offered four million dollars each, Paul Newman, Robert Redford, and Steve Mc-Queen all turned down the role of Superman. It eventually went to Christopher Reeve who was paid $250,000.

Gary Cooper believed *Gone With the Wind* would be "the biggest flop in Hollywood's history," and turned down the leading role as Rhett Butler.

Bing Crosby turned down the role of Columbo in the eponymous TV detective series before Peter Falk was offered the part.

The role that made Peter O'Toole a star, Lawrence of Arabia, had been turned down by Marlon Brando and Albert Finney.

Peter Ustinov was signed for the part of Inspector Jacques Clousseau but pulled out at the last minute, opening the way for Peter Sellers to play the part.

Doris Day turned down the role of Mrs. Robinson in *The Graduate* in 1967 because she said she could not picture herself making love on a film set. Anne Bancroft was given the role and was hugely successful.

Spencer Tracy said he would only take the part of the Penguin in the *Batman* TV series if he was allowed to kill Batman.

After turning down the role of Marshall Matt Dylan in the TV show *Gunsmoke*, John Wayne recommended his good friend James Arness for the part. It made him famous.

Charles Bronson and James Coburn both turned down the part of the "Man with No Name" in the spaghetti Western *A Fistful of Dollars* before Clint Eastwood was signed for the role.

Lucille Ball was thrown out of the New York Robert Minton–John Murray Anderson School of Drama at the age of fifteen because her instructor thought she was "too quiet and shy."

ODD JOBS

Maisie Wilmar-Brown, the wardrobe mistress for the Agatha Christie play *The Mousetrap*, ironed more than thirty-six miles of shirts in the years between 1952 until her death in 1973.

Errol Flynn once won thirty thousand dollars answering questions on sailing on the 1950s television quiz show *The Big Surprise*.

As a young actor James Dean earned money for food by testing stunts for the TV show *Beat the Clock*.

Sylvester Stallone used to sweep the lion cages in

New York City's Central Park Zoo to pay his way while trying to break into acting.

Alan Ladd had a hot-dog stall known as "Tiny's"—he was only five feet, six inches tall—before breaking into films.

Margaret Hamilton, the Wicked Witch of the West in *The Wizard of Oz*, was once a kindergarten teacher.

Sean Connery once worked as a coffin polisher.

BIG BREAKS

Shirley Temple was only three years old when she appeared in her first film, crime drama *The Red-Haired Alibi*.

Goldie Hawn's career as an actress-comedienne was launched after being spotted as a dancer in the chorus line on *The Andy Griffith Show* in 1966.

Anthony Quinn got his first film part in the 1937 film *The Plainsman* by pretending to be a Cheyenne Indian.

Margaret Rutherford's stage debut at the age of thirty-three was as a long-nosed fairy in a pantomime called *Little Jack Horner*.

Actor David Niven made his screen debut as a Mexican, wearing a blanket, in the very first *Hopalong Cassidy* movie.

James Stewart played the accordion in a tearoom before being offered his first part in a Broadway play. He showed off his little-known skill in the 1955 film *The Man from Laramie*.

When Otto Preminger hired Kim Novak from Columbia Pictures for a hundred thousand dollars to use her in his film *The Man with the Golden Arm*, she was still only paid a hundred dollars a week.

In 1976 Sarah Caldwell became the first woman to conduct the Metropolitan Opera in New York City.

Pia Zadora's first movie role was as a young child protagonist in *Santa Claus Conquers the Martians*.

In her first television appearance in 1954, Lauren Bacall recited the poem "Casey at the Bat."

After Harrison Ford's brief 1966 appearance as a bellboy in *Dead Heat on a Merry-Go-Round* he was told, "Kid, you ain't got it."

Boris Karloff's first film role was as a five-dollar-a-day extra (a Mexican soldier) in a 1919 nonhorror silent movie *His Majesty the American*.

Actors Studio legend Lee Strasberg said that the two students of his who stood out from the rest were Marilyn Monroe and Marlon Brando.

The man who became president of Kenya, Jomo Kenyatta, played a tribal chief in the 1935 British film *Sanders of the River*.

HEARD BUT NOT SEEN

When a scene featuring Laurence Olivier was restored for the 1991 rerelease of the 1960 film *Spartacus*, Olivier was already dead. His voice was dubbed by Anthony Hopkins.

Johnny Mathis dubbed Miss Piggy's singing voice in *The Muppet Movie*.

The longest list of film credits on record before *The Matrix Reloaded* was for the 1988 film *Who Framed Roger Rabbit?* There were 763 names. It might have been 764 but Kathleen Turner, who dubbed the voice of Jessica Rabbit, asked not to be included in the credits.

Mel Blanc, the voice of Bugs Bunny, was allergic to carrots.

Debra Winger was the voice of E.T.

CARTOON CORNUCOPIA

The Bugs Bunny prototype first appeared in the cartoon *Porky's Hair Hunt* in 1938.

Artists had to draw 6,469,952 spots for the 1961 Walt Disney animated film *One Hundred and One Dalmatians*.

All of the characters in *The Flintstones* had four fingers on each hand and three toes on each foot.

CELEBRITY RELATIONS

Debbie Reynolds's daughter, Carrie Fisher, once said, "I always wanted to do what my mother did. Get all dressed up—shoot people—fall in the mud. I never considered doing anything else."

In pop royalty, the Queen of Blues is Dinah Washington, the Queen of Soul is Aretha Franklin, the Queen of Disco is Donna Summer, the King of Swing is Benny Goodman, the King of the Cowboys is Roy Rogers, and the King is Elvis Presley.

Burt Reynolds now lives in what was once the Florida holiday home of Chicago gangster Al Capone.

The actor who played the T-1000 in *Terminator 2*, Robert Patrick, is the brother of the lead singer of Filter.

Marlon Brando, Mel Gibson, Clark Gable, and Errol Flynn have all played Fletcher Christian in *Mutiny on the Bounty*.

Howard Taylor (brother of Elizabeth) was so determined not to take a screen test arranged by his pushy, stage-struck mother that he shaved his head the night before the test.

When President Ronald Reagan began using the term *Star Wars* to describe his computer-controlled space-defense system, George Lucas launched a lawsuit against him to protect his film title.

When in 1986 Joan Rivers appeared on national TV with Victoria Principal, with whom she'd had a long-standing feud, the comedienne deliberately gave out the actress's unpublished home telephone number.

Rudolph Nureyev once danced a pas de deux from *Swan Lake* with Miss Piggy on *The Muppet Show*.

The longest swordfight on film, lasting six and a half minutes, was between Stewart Granger and Mel Ferrer in the 1952 film *Scaramouche*.

The part of outlaw Jesse James has been played by many great Hollywood stars, but the first actor ever to play the role on screen was James's own son, Jesse James Jr., in the 1921 silent movie *Under the Black Flag*.

Liquid Paper was invented by the mother of Mike Nesmith of the Monkees.

Paul McCartney's mother was a midwife.

Don McLean's famous song "American Pie" was inspired by the name of the plane in which Buddy Holly died—American Pie.

Al Capone was so pleased with the 1932 film *Scarface* that he gave director Howard Hawks a miniature machine gun as a thank-you present.

Elton John's uncle was a professional soccer player. He broke his leg while playing for Nottingham Forest in the 1959 FA Cup final.

Keith Moon of The Who inspired the Muppet drummer Animal.

🌰 WHEN STARS ALIGN

Michael Caine fell in love with a woman he saw in a Maxwell House coffee commercial. She was Shakira Baksh, whom he later married.

Catherine Deneuve had a son by Roger Vadim and a daughter by Marcello Mastroianni but was married to neither.

Under the Motion Picture censorship code, which was effective from 1934 to 1968, a screen kiss could only last thirty seconds before being labeled "indecent."

The word *pregnant* was banned by censors from the script of the TV sitcom *I Love Lucy* in 1952—even though Lucy was obviously expecting, and her son's birth was a major feature in that season's episodes.

Popeye's girlfriend, Olive Oyl, wore a size 14A shoe.

The first TV sitcom couple to share a double bed was the Munsters, Lily and Herman, during the 1964–5 season.

Ronald Reagan and his second wife, Nancy Davis, appeared opposite each other in the movie *Hellcats of the Navy*.

Tom Selleck, who played heartthrob Thomas Magnum in the TV series *Magnum, P.I.*, was not chosen by the girl when he appeared as a contestant on *The Dating Game*.

SCANDALOUS STARS

Actress Joan Collins was fifty years old when she posed seminude for *Playboy* magazine. It was a sell-out edition.

The first time Madonna appeared on the *Late Show with David Letterman*, her foul language had to be bleeped out twelve times. On her second appearance it only happened once.

The BBC once rejected a claim that Chuck Berry's 1972 hit song "My Ding-a-Ling" (the tale of a young man who couldn't stop playing with the song-title object and invited his friends to join in) was intended to stimulate self- and mutual-masturbation. Quoting Chuck Berry, they said the record was plainly about a boy who was given a bell to play with.

David Selznick, producer of *Gone With the Wind*, was fined five thousand dollars by the Motion Picture Association of America for letting the word *damn* be used.

The Muppet Show was banned from television in Saudi Arabia because one of its stars was Miss Piggy. Pigs are forbidden to Muslims.

Mia Farrow once gave her vital statistics as 20–20–20.

The Cotton Club was involved in so many lawsuits before its release in 1984 that the director included the name of the winning lawyers on the closing credits.

The only X-rated film ever to win an Oscar for Best Picture was *Midnight Cowboy*. It was later reduced to an R rating.

WORDS TO LIVE BY

When a reporter asked pioneer chat-show host Johnny Carson what he would like his epitaph to be, he replied, "I'll be right back."

The late W. C. Fields once said that any man who hated children and dogs couldn't be all bad. He probably turned in his grave when, in 1980, his home was sold to make way for a nursery school.

Marilyn Monroe's last ever line in a film was "How do you find your way back in the dark?" spoken to Clark Gable in *The Misfits*.

STAR TREK-KING

In the early episodes of *Star Trek*, Dr. McCoy's medical scanner was just an ordinary salt shaker.

Leonard Nimoy, who went on to play Mr. Spock in *Star Trek*, first appeared in alien guise in the pilot of a TV science-fiction series, *The Zombie Vanguard*. He played a Martian in the zombie army.

Spot, Mr. Data's cat in *Star Trek: The Next Generation*, was played by six different cats.

The initial *T* in *Star Trek* Captain James T. Kirk's name stands for Tiberius.

MILESTONES

The most expensive silent movie ever made was the 1926 epic *Ben Hur*, which cost $3.9 million.

The first video ever played on MTV Europe was "Money for Nothing" by Dire Straits.

The term *rock 'n' roll* was coined in 1951.

The first custard pie ever thrown on-screen was in the 1950s silent comedy *Keystone Kops*, where Mabel Normand threw a pie at Ben Turpin.

To open their first ever theater in 1903 in New Castle, Pennsylvania, the Warner brothers, Jack, Harry, Sam, and Albert, borrowed the ninety-nine chairs they needed from the local undertaker, which had to be taken back later for funerals.

Only one woman, Tracy Reed, appeared in Stanley Kubrick's *Dr. Strangelove or: How I Learned to Stop Worrying and Love the Bomb*.

MGM's first picture with sound, the 1928 *White Shadows in the South Seas*, had only one word of dialogue: "Hello."

More extras were used in the 1981 film *Gandhi* than in any other movie; three hundred thousand were used for only a ten-minute funeral sequence.

Charlie Chaplin died on Christmas Day in 1977.

Lucille Ball did not become a redhead until the age of thirty—after twelve years as a platinum blonde and eighteen years as a natural brunette.

The first film to be released in CinemaScope in 1953 was *The Robe*.

Because D. W. Griffith wanted one of his stars in the 1916 silent film *Intolerance* to have eyelashes that brushed her cheeks, false eyelashes were invented.

The calabash pipe, most often associated with Sherlock Holmes, was not used to portray him until William Gillette (an American) played him onstage. Gillette needed a pipe he could keep in his mouth while he spoke his lines.

Jean Harlow was the first actress to appear on the cover of *Life* magazine.

Gene Autry was the only entertainer to have all five stars on Hollywood's Walk of Fame—that is, one for each of the five categories of film, TV, recording, radio, and theater.

According to Warner Brothers, Sam Peckinpah used more ammunition—ninety thousand blank rounds—than the entire Mexican Revolution when he made *The Wild Bunch*.

There are 1,943 names listed in the closing credits of *The Matrix Reloaded*.

The phrase *cameo role* was invented by Mike Todd when he made *Around the World in Eighty Days* in 1955. He had a host of top Hollywood stars playing bit parts.

◣ SPEAKING OF CAMEOS

In the movie *The Right Stuff*, there is a scene where a government recruiter for the Mercury Astronaut Program, played by Jeff Goldblum, is in a bar at Muroc Dry Lake, California. His partner suggests legendary jet test pilot Chuck Yeager as a good astronaut candidate. Goldblum proceeds to badmouth Yeager, claiming they need someone who went to college. During this conversation the real Chuck Yeager is playing the bartender, who is standing behind the recruiters and eavesdropping. General Yeager is listed low in the movie's credits as "Fred."

THE MAKING OF . . .

Wayne's World was filmed in two weeks.

As part of his fee for appearing in *Terminator 2*, Arnold Schwarzenegger was given a Gulf Stream GIII jet aircraft.

The blood in the famous shower scene in Alfred Hitchcock's *Psycho* was in fact Hershey's chocolate syrup.

In *The Adventures of Robin Hood*, Olivia de Havilland rode the horse that later found fame as famous cowboy steed Trigger.

The legs shown walking down the street in the opening of *Saturday Night Fever* were not John Travolta's but those of his stand-in, Jeff Zinn.

Sam Goldwyn spent an extra twenty thousand dollars reshooting a scene in *Bulldog Drummond* because he didn't understand the word *din*. He had the word *noise* substituted.

In film-editing, lingo, R2-D2—the robot in *Star Wars*—means Reel 2, Dialogue 2.

Telly Savalas first shaved his head not for the role of Kojak but for the part of Pontius Pilate in *The Greatest Story Ever Told*.

The snow scenes in the film *It's a Wonderful Life* were shot during a record heat wave in Southern California.

In all his film contracts James Stewart was granted the right to select all the hats he would wear on-screen.

The race around the Great Court at Trinity College, Cambridge, featured in the 1981 film *Chariots of Fire* was actually filmed at Eton College because the Trinity dons refused to acknowledge the movie in any way.

In a two-hour movie there are 10,800 feet of film.

Roger Moore has it written into all his film contracts that he must be provided with an unlimited supply of hand-rolled Cuban cigars during filming.

In *Psycho* the color of Mrs. Bates's dress is periwinkle blue.

A real cruise liner, the *Isle de France*, was deliberately sunk to provide the dramatic climax to the film *The Last Voyage* in 1960.

The name of the ship in which Dr. Doolittle sailed in the 1967 film was the *Flounder*.

The nineteen-foot-long Batmobile used in the TV series *Batman*, starring Adam West, got only four miles to the gallon.

Three thousand rats were specially bred for the film *Indiana Jones and the Last Crusade*.

The license plate number of the General Lee in *The Dukes of Hazzard* is CNH 320.

ECCENTRIC ENTERTAINERS

Actor John Barrymore kept a pet vulture named Maloney, which would sit on his knee and hiss.

Irish-born actor Peter O'Toole claims he is never without his emerald green socks.

Silent-movie star Ben Turpin had a hundred-thousand-dollar insurance policy covering his trademark crossed eyes.

Shirley Temple always had fifty-six curls in her hair.

Senator Barry Goldwater attended the opening-night ceremonies and festivities at Bugsy Siegel's famous Las Vegas casino. He was hopping mad when they left him out of the movie *Bugsy*.

Michael Jackson owns the rights to the South Carolina state anthem.

Sean Connery has to have the tattoos on his arm covered by makeup when filming. The tattoos declare his love for his mom and dad, and for Scotland, which he represented in the 1952 Mr. Universe contest.

Fred Astaire had his legs insured for a mere hundred thousand dollars while his dancing partner, Cyd Charise, had hers covered for almost seven million dollars.

Actress Farrah Fawcett had a tap named after her—the gold-plated Farrah Faucet.

The Beatles song "Martha My Dear" was written by Paul McCartney about his sheepdog.

Walt Disney had wooden teeth.

WHAT WAS THE OTHER HALF WATCHING?

Half the world's population has seen at least one James Bond movie.

THE END, TAKE 2

The real Butch Cassidy did not die in Bolivia but returned home, minus the Sundance Kid, and became an adding-machine manufacturer.

ROWDY ROYALS

WEDDED BLISS?

According to the Bible, King Solomon had seven hundred wives.

ROYAL REAL ESTATE

The Queen has ten residences available to her if necessary: Buckingham Palace, Windsor Castle, St. James's Palace, Kensington Palace, Hampton Court palace, Balmoral, Sandringham, Holyrood House, the Tower of London, and the Palace of Westminster.

MODERN MONARCHS

The current Queen was born on a Wednesday.

The Queen has a special car mascot—a silver model of St. George and the Dragon—which is transferred to any royal car in which she is traveling.

The Queen is an excellent mimic and sometimes entertains the family by aping the prime ministers she has known in the last half century.

The Queen always writes with a fountain pen that belonged to her father, King George VI.

The Queen's racing colors are red and blue.

The last time the Queen curtsied was in 1952—to her father's body in St. George's Chapel, Windsor.

The Queen Mother could play the bongo drums expertly.

The Queen Mother suffered from whooping cough on her honeymoon.

Sometimes Prince Philip hides a radio in his top hat when he attends the Ascot races—because he hates racing and prefers to listen to the cricket matches.

Prince Philip keeps a collection of press cartoons of himself on the walls of his lavatory in Sandringham.

Within minutes of delivering a speech on road safety in 1957, Prince Philip crashed his car.

Prince Philip wears contact lenses.

Queen Mary turned up at a 1938 Buckingham Palace party wearing five diamond necklaces at the same time.

Princess Margaret was afraid of the dark.

Prince Andrew refused to wear shorts under his kilt as a child to be like Prince Philip. "Papa doesn't wear anything and neither shall I!" he would cry.

Princess Diana was the first royal bride not to use the word *obey* in her marriage vows.

Princess Diana was a very enthusiastic tap dancer.

After meeting the duke of Kent, jazz musician Louis Armstrong sent him a twenty-first birthday message in which he wrote, "To Black Jack, the sharpest little cat I know. Satch."

There is a secret station on the London Underground system beneath Buckingham Palace, so that the family can escape to Heathrow Airport in an emergency.

CHECKING ON CHARLES

Prince Charles used the pickup line "I like to give myself heirs" when he attended Cambridge University. Prince William's pickup line at St. Andrew's University was "I'm the next king. Wanna pull?"

President Richard Nixon tried to marry off the then-twenty-three-year-old Prince Charles to his daughter Tricia. Nixon and his wife even went to the extent of deliberately leaving the couple alone in rooms at the White House, so they could get "better acquainted."

In official photographs for their wedding stamps, Prince Charles stood on a soapbox to give the impression he was much taller than Diana. For their engagement pictures, Diana was made to stand on a lower step of stairs.

Prince Charles twice failed his maths "O" level.

Prince Charles's first Shetland pony was called Fum.

Prince Charles would sometimes adopt the name Charlie Chester when signing himself into clubs.

GOOD QUEEN BESS

In her sixties, Queen Elizabeth I often sat in front of her whole court with her dress thrown open at the front to expose her breasts. No reason was ever given for this amazing royal display.

Queen Elizabeth I banned all mirrors from the royal apartments during the last decade of her life.

Queen Elizabeth I had more than two thousand dresses.

The bishop of London had one of his own sound teeth extracted to show Queen Elizabeth I how easily one of her own rotten teeth could be removed.

I AM HENRY THE EIGHTH, I AM

The heart of King Henry VIII's beheaded wife, Anne Boleyn, was buried separately from her body in a church in Suffolk.

Anne of Cleves looked so different from her portraits that King Henry VIII asked his courtiers, "Have you brought me the Flanders mare?"

Henry VIII's longest marriage was to Catherine of Aragon, his first bride. It lasted twenty-three years and eleven months. His shortest was to Anne of Cleves. The marriage ended in divorce after six months.

ROYAL TRADITION

It is a popular misconception that the royal family cannot vote in political elections. It is only the Queen, herself, who is not allowed to vote. Other members of the family merely choose not to.

All royal babies are baptized with water brought from the River Jordan.

VICTORIA'S SECRETS

Queen Victoria adopted the nickname Pussy for her eldest daughter, the Princess Royal.

Queen Victoria often put on a Scottish accent when traveling north of the border.

Queen Victoria described votes for women as "a mad, wicked folly."

Queen Victoria was taught to sing by the composer Mendelssohn.

Queen Victoria told her eldest daughter, when she became pregnant, "It really is too dreadful to have the first year of one's married life and happiness spoilt by discomfort and misery—I was furious at being in that position."

Queen Victoria refused to believe in the existence of lesbianism and scratched out all reference to sex between women in the antihomosexuality bill before she signed it. That is why female homosexuality was never prosecuted in Britain.

Queen Victoria was the first woman to use chloroform during childbirth.

Queen Victoria's funeral was the first royal funeral to be held during the day and the first to involve pageantry. Previous royal funerals had taken place at night and were strictly private affairs.

ROYALLY QUOTED

In his personal prayer book, King George III struck out the words *our most religious and gracious king* and substituted *a most miserable sinner.*

An aide announced Napoleon's death to King George IV in 1821 with, "Your greatest enemy is dead, sir." The king replied, "By God, is she?" believing his aid was referring to the Queen.

King George V described his ancestors, buried in St George's Chapel, Windsor, as "a strange busload to be traveling through eternity together."

Discussing public duty, Princess Anne said, "There is a limit to how interesting a forty acre field can be, in my opinion."

The Queen's description of Niagara Falls: "It looks very damp."

The Queen's nickname for her grandfather King George VI was "Grandpapa England."

The Queen Mother used to describe her clothes as "my props."

Not a lover of the arts, King George II would frequently scream in his thickly accented English: "No more bainting, blays, or boetry."

When Lord Harris first turned up at Ascot wearing his now famous trademark tweed, King Edward VII greeted him with, "Mornin', Harris, going rattin'?"

Prince Philip once remarked, "Constitutionally, I don't exist."

King Edward VII's favorite dog, Ceasar, had "I am Ceasar—the King's Dog" on his collar.

Prime Minister Gladstone said of King Edward VII: "He knows everything except what is in books."

Princess Anne said at an American press conference in 1975: "Everything I've seen written thus far is a copy of every falsification I've ever seen written about me. Even the pictures are not of me."

Princess Anne once said she would like to have been a long-distance lorry driver.

In dire financial straits, when a teenager, the Queen Mother sent her father a telegram message reading, "S.O.S., L.S.D., R.S.V.P."

◗ ROYAL RECORDS

The longest British reign was that of Queen Victoria, who was on the throne sixty-three years and seven months from 1837 to 1901. The shortest reign was that of Lady Jane Grey, which lasted only nine days in 1553. She was only sixteen when she was beheaded.

The British monarch with the largest number of illegitimate children was King Henry I with twenty-one. King Charles II was a worthy runner-up with fifteen.

The English Queen with the most Christian names was Mary, wife of King George V, who had eight: Victoria Mary Augusta Louisa Olga Pauline Claudine Agnes.

In the past millennium there have been three occasions when three kings ruled in a single year—1066 (Edward the Confessor, King Harold, and King William the Conqueror), 1483 (Edward IV, Edward V, and Richard III), and 1936 (George V, Edward VIII, and George VI).

NOT QUITE "YOUR MAJESTY"

When they made Prince Charles an honorary chieftain, the Kainai tribe of Alberta, Canada, gave him the name of Prince Red Chow.

Prince Andrew was nicknamed the "sniggerer" by his schoolmates at Gordonstoun. At the same school, Prince Edward was nicknamed "Jaws" because of the metal braces on his teeth.

At Timbertops school in Australia, Prince Charles was nicknamed "Pommy Bastard."

Prince Charles was named Hooligan of the Year in 1978 by the RSPCA after he had hunted boar in Liechtenstein.

King William IV of England was also King William III of Scotland, William II of Ireland, and King William I of Hanover.

King George IV's nickname for his much unloved wife, Queen Caroline, was the Fiend.

The Queen named one of her horses "Charlton" after brothers Bobby and Jackie, who helped lead England to victory in the 1966 World Cup.

Nell Gwynne always referred to her lover, King Charles II, as Charles the third. Her previous two lovers had also been called Charles.

NOBLE DEATHS

King Edward III died of gonorrhea, which he caught from his mistress when he was sixty-five years of age. Henry VIII and Edward VI also died of venereal disease. George IV and William IV both died of cirrhosis of the liver.

So anxious was he not to shiver with cold lest people think him to be trembling with fear, King Charles I wore two shirts for his execution.

The *Times* obituary of King George IV reported, "There never was an individual less regretted by his fellow creatures than this deceased king."

ROYALLY ECCENTRIC

King George V banned his son, King Edward VIII, for a year from playing billiards, after he miscued and slit the cloth on the table.

King Charles I's favorite joke was to place his court dwarf, Jeffrey Hudson, who was eighteen inches tall, between two halves of a loaf of bread and pretend to eat him.

It is said that King James I became a lifelong heavy drinker because his wet nurse was an alcoholic and he received such copious quantities of the hard stuff through her milk.

After the duke died the duchess of Windsor always kept a loaded pistol by her bedside.

The duchess of Wurttemberg had her spectacles accidentally knocked off during the wedding banquet for Prince Philip's parents. When she lashed out with her handbag in furious retaliation, she hit the wrong person over the head.

King James I joined his friend Philip Herbert and his bride in bed on their honeymoon night.

King George I of Greece used the huge ballroom of his Athens palace as a roller skating ring.

In Balmoral, Princess Margaret dressed up as Last of the Red Hot Mamas, Sophie Tucker, to give a birthday party impersonation.

Even when they dined without guests, King George V insisted his sons wear full evening dress—white tie, tails, and decorations, including the garter star and sash.

King Edward VIII was an accomplished banjo player. He could also play the ukulele and once composed and played a tune on the bagpipes.

King Edward VII had an American bowling alley installed at Sandringham.

As a prince, King Edward VI had a "whipping boy" named Barnaby Fitzpatrick, who was beaten every time the prince misbehaved during lessons.

To prevent her secrets being revealed to snoopers the Queen always uses black blotting paper.

Richard II once had to pawn his crown because he was such a spendthrift.

Princess Augusta of Saxe-Gotha was physically sick during her wedding to Frederick, prince of Wales in 1736.

The sirloin was introduced when King James I knighted a joint of beef (a loin), which was particularly tasty.

ROYALLY ACCOMPLISHED

Eton College was founded by King Henry VI in 1440.

In the seventeenth century, King Charles II twice won the Newmarket Cup, riding his own horse.

Prince Philip quit smoking on the night before his wedding.

The Theatre Royal in Drury Lane was founded by King Charles II in 1663.

King Richard II invented the handkerchief.

ROYAL TIES

Henry II's second wife, Eleanor, was forty when their first child was born.

George VI, George V, Charles I, and Henry VIII were all second sons who succeeded to the throne.

The Queen and Prince Philip are third cousins through their descent from Queen Victoria and are also related through King George III and King Christian IX of Denmark.

ROYALLY SCANDALOUS

Prince Philip gave away television personality Hèléne Cordet at her wedding, and became godfather to both her children—not surprisingly raising suggestions that they were his own.

King Edward I was forty years older than his second wife, Margaret.

Six of Britain's kings were homosexuals. They were William II, Richard I, Edward II, Richard II, James I, and William III.

William of Orange was four inches shorter than his wife, Queen Mary.

King Charles II's coronation was delayed because there was no regalia. Oliver Cromwell had sold it all and it had to be replaced.

After they had run a series of revealing palace stories, Prince Philip described the *Daily Express* as "a bloody awful newspaper. It is full of lies, scandal, and imagination. It is a vicious newspaper."

The last widowed queen of England to remarry was Queen Catherine Parr, who married Lord Seymoor in 1547—her fourth husband.

NOT QUITE ROYAL ENOUGH

King Edward V reigned only three months in 1483 before being deposed. He was never crowned. His descendant, King Edward VIII, was also never crowned. He abdicated before his coronation had been due to take place.

SCIENCE CENTER

ANIMAL INSTINCTS

In the last three thousand years, no new animals have been domesticated.

Since 1600 a total of 109 species and subspecies of bird have become extinct.

A bird has to fly at a minimum speed of eleven miles per hour to be able to keep itself aloft.

The Arctic tern enjoys more daylight hours than any other living creature. Each year it spends four months of constant daylight in the Arctic before swimming south to spend four months of constant daylight in the Antarctic. It makes the twenty-thousand-mile return trip every year.

The eyes of some birds weigh more than their brains.

More than a thousand birds a year die from smashing into windows.

The two-foot-long New Zealand mountain bird kea likes to eat the strips of rubber around car windows.

A robin's egg is blue, but if you put it in vinegar for thirty days it turns yellow.

In 1872 locals in North Yorkshire recorded that a swarm of ladybirds took three days to pass.

Baby robins eat fourteen feet of earthworms a day.

Roosters cannot crow if they are not able to fully extend their necks.

The difference between fowl and poultry is that poultry are domesticated fowl.

An ostrich's eye is bigger than its brain.

To keep cool, ostriches urinate on their legs. The urine then evaporates like sweat.

The longest recorded flight of a chicken was thirteen seconds.

Scientists in Canada discovered during tests that

chickens increase their egg output when pop music is being played.

Emus have double-plumed feathers and they lay emerald to forest green eggs. Emus and kangaroos cannot walk backward, and for that reason they are featured on the Australian coat of arms.

A great horned owl can turn its head 270 degrees.

Owls are the only birds that can see the color blue.

Crows have the largest cerebral hemispheres relative to their body size of any avian family.

If you feed a seagull Alka Seltzer its stomach will explode.

A pelican can hold about twenty-five pounds of fish in its pouch.

The sparrow was imported to New York in 1850 to cope with an excess of tree worms.

Bowerbirds of Australia and New Guinea decorate their courting grounds with everything from beetle wings to car keys.

No one knows why a duck's quack doesn't echo.

When penguins hop onto an ice floe they always choose one that will take them back to land.

The archerfish brings down its insect prey with well-aimed mouthfuls of spit. It is even able to compensate for refraction when it shoots from under water.

A shark is the only fish that can blink with both eyes.

A shrimp's heart is in its head.

Every night the parrot fish sleeps inside a mucus cocoon, which it constructs daily to block its body smell from predators.

A whale's penis is called a dork.

An adult electric eel can produce up to six hundred volts—sufficient to stun a grown horse.

The California sea otter grasps its mate's nose in its teeth while copulating.

The sperm whale's brain weighs up to twenty pounds, which is six times heavier than a human's and is the heaviest of all the mammals.

A starfish doesn't have a brain.

You can tell the age of a fish by the number of growth rings on each of its scales.

The oldest-known goldfish lived to forty-one years of age. Its name was Fred.

A humpback whale's milk is 54 percent fat.

The smallest fish in the world is the Trimattum Nanus of the Chagos Archipelago. It measures just 0.33 inches long.

The blood of an octopus is pale bluish green.

The first fish in space was a South American guppy in 1976.

A type of jellyfish found off the coast of England is the longest animal in the world.

Jellyfish are the wettest creatures on earth, being made up of 95.4 percent water. An average adult human has a water content of just over 60 percent.

If the eggs spawned by all the female cod in one season survived, they would fill the oceans from seabed to surface. Cod lay between four and five million eggs at a time—but usually only about five survive.

Flying fish "fly" at between thirty-five and forty-five miles per hour.

Sharks can detect the heartbeats of other fish.

A shark can detect one part of blood in 100 million parts of water.

The northern fur seal has more mates each year than any other mammal. The average male will mate with between forty and sixty females each season.

The 2.5-ton, fifty-five-foot-long giant squid has the largest eyes of any animal on earth, each being more than a foot in diameter.

You can tell the sex of a crab by its stomach: the female's is beehive-shaped, while the male's is lighthouse-shaped.

One way to tell seals and sea lions apart is that sea lions have external ears and testicles.

Orcas kill sharks by torpedoing into the shark's stomach from underneath, causing the shark to explode.

The only way to stop the pain of a flathead fish's sting is by rubbing its slime on the wound it gave you.

The common goldfish is the only animal that can see both infrared and ultraviolet light.

In the Caribbean there are oysters that can climb trees.

The oldest tortoise lived to the age of 152.

Even with its favorite food laid out to tempt it, a giant tortoise can manage a top speed of only five yards a minute—0.17 miles per hour.

You can tell a turtle's gender by the noise it makes: males grunt, females hiss.

The rattlesnake has the best heat-detecting equipment in nature. Using the two organs between its eyes and nostrils it can locate a mouse by its body heat at a distance of fifteen miles.

Vets at the London Zoo once fitted a snake with a glass eye.

Crocodiles cannot stick their tongues out.

Alligators cannot move backward.

An iguana can hold its breath for twenty-eight minutes.

Iguanas, koalas, and Komodo dragons all have two penises.

A grass snake can move at 4.2 miles per hour.

When female elephants have been pregnant for more than twenty months and are still not in labor they will travel a hundred miles searching for the leaves of the Boraginaceae tree—which can also induce birth in humans.

The tip of an elephant's trunk is so sensitive and flexible that it can pick up a pin.

Most elephants weigh less than the tongue of the blue whale.

An elephant can smell water three miles away.

In a dental experiment on elephants, motorcar tires were chopped up and baked in their bread. The elephants never noticed.

An elephant's trunk can hold four gallons of water.

Murphy Oil Soap is the chemical most commonly used to clean elephants.

In 1902 the British horse population was three and a half million. It required fifteen million acres to provide their food and they produced ten million tons of manure a year.

Neither horses nor rabbits can vomit.

Mill Reef, the famous racehorse, received more than thirty get-well cards a day after fracturing a foreleg.

The underside of a horse's hoof is called a frog. The frog peels off several times a year to be replaced by a new growth.

The so-called "wild" horses of North America are actually feral animals—free-living descendants of domestic horses that escaped or were turned loose.

A quarter of all mammal species are bats.

The world's smallest mammal is the bumblebee bat of Thailand, weighing less than a penny.

Some carnivores, rodents, bats, and insectivores have a penis bone called a baculum.

The one-ounce brown bat, which is most common in North America, is capable of eating five hundred insects an hour during its nighttime feeding.

Armadillos and humans are the only animals that can get leprosy.

Armadillos have four babies at a time and they are always all the same sex.

Armadillos can walk under water.

Armadillos can be housebroken.

> The anteater, aardvark, spiny anteater, and scaly anteater are completely unrelated. In fact, the closest relatives to anteaters are sloths and armadillos. The closest relative to the spiny anteater is the platypus, and the aardvark is in an order all by itself.

The sloth can starve to death even with a plentiful supply of food if there are too many cloudy days in a row. It needs sunshine to raise its body temperature so that the bacteria in its stomach are warm enough to digest the food it eats. It can take up to four days to digest even a single stomachful of food.

> A rhinoceros has three toes encased in a hoof on each foot.

Rhinos belong to the same family as horses and are thought to have inspired the myth of the unicorn.

> Hippopotamuses make 80 percent of their vocalizations under water.

The largest order of mammals is rodents with about seventeen hundred species.

> A rat can chew through just about any building material, including concrete.

A rat can survive longer without water than a camel.

As of 2002, rats in New York City outnumbered humans by twelve to one.

In a single night a mole can tunnel 220 feet.

Hamsters love to eat crickets.

Most hamsters blink one eye at a time.

In Australia, the male antechinus mouse has up to sixteen partners per sex session, which take place in trees and can last up to twelve hours. Often they become so weak they fall out of the trees and are killed.

THIS LITTLE PIGGY

The world's pig population is approximately 857,100,000.

A pig always sleeps on its right side.

A pig's orgasm lasts for thirty minutes.

A gruntle is the best word to describe the snout of a pig.

A pig's skin is thickest on its back, where it can be up to one-sixth-inch thick.

The brachiosaurus had a heart the size of a pickup truck.

Twelve or more cows are known as a flink.

The black-and-white spots of Holstein dairy cattle are like fingerprints: no two cows have the same pattern of spots.

Cows experience flatulence sixteen times a day and produce around sixty-five pounds of manure.

When you cross cattle with buffalo you get a beefalo.

It is illegal in Alaska to give a moose an alcoholic drink.

The cells that make up the antlers of a moose are the fastest-growing animal cells in nature.

The longest recorded life span of a camel was thirty-five years and five months.

Camel milk is the only milk that doesn't curdle when boiled.

A full-grown bear can run as fast as a horse over short distances.

The opening to the cave in which a bear hibernates is always on a northern slope.

The British Goat Society was formed in 1879.

You can tell the age of a mountain goat by the number of rings on its small black horns.

A lion's roar can be heard from five miles away.

The muzzle of a lion is like a fingerprint: no two lions have the same pattern of whiskers.

When a chimpanzee's daubed prints were submitted in a test folio in Pretoria in place of a student's work, they were given a pass mark by the examiners.

Human birth-control pills work on gorillas.

Spider monkeys like banana daiquiris.

The honey badger can withstand hundreds of African bee stings that would kill any other animal.

Other than humans, black lemurs are the only primates that may have blue eyes.

Rabbits can run at up to forty-five miles per hour.

Shrews and platypuses are the only mammals that are poisonous.

Some female hyenas have a pseudopenis.

Ferrets can sleep for up to twenty hours a day.

The wolverine is the largest member of the weasel family.

A hedgehog's heart beats three hundred times a minute on average.

A tiger's paw prints are called pug marks.

Giraffes have no vocal cords.

Jackals have one more pair of chromosomes than dogs or wolves.

INSECT ASIDE

Eighty percent of the world's food crops are pollinated by insects.

An estimated 80 percent of animals on earth have six legs.

Mosquitoes are attracted to the color blue more than twice as much as to any other single color.

There are more beetles than any other creature in the world.

The average caterpillar has 248 muscles in its head.

The mayfly lives only six hours, but its eggs take three years to hatch.

Only two animal species wage war on their own kind—ants and humans.

Termites eat through wood twice as fast when listening to rock music.

A bumblebee beats its wings 160 times a second.

The only insect that can turn its head is a praying mantis.

The common garden worm has five pairs of hearts.

A male emperor moth can smell a female up to seven miles away.

One Australian wasp has the scientific name *Aha ha*.

Slugs travel at a top speed of .007 miles per hour, can stretch to eleven times their length, and have twenty-seven thousand teeth to help eat their food.

A female bed bug has survived 565 days without food.

In England it was once considered sacrilege to kill a bee, which was regarded as the holiest of insects.

A snail can sleep for three years.

Moths hear through the hairs on their bodies.

The average housefly lives for one month.

In his book *The Insects* naturalist Url N. Lanham reports that the aphid reproduction cycle is so rapid that the females are born pregnant.

A dragonfly has a lifespan of just twenty-four hours.

A South American termite queen can produce thirty thousand eggs in a day and do this daily for up to a year. A colony of more than five million termites can come from a single queen.

The world's termites outweigh the world's humans by ten to one.

The longest recorded lifespan of a slug is eighteen months.

Some ribbon worms will eat themselves if they cannot find food.

Most spiders have eight eyes.

Spiders do not get caught in their own webs because they cover themselves with a greasy antisilk film.

Depending on the type of grasshopper, its "ears" are located either on its forelegs or on the base of its abdomen.

Honeybees have hair on their eyes.

Ants cannot chew their food; they move their jaws sideways like scissors to extract juices from it.

Jumping spiders have been found at a height of twenty-two thousand feet on Mount Everest.

The majority of spiders belong to the "orb weaver" spider family Aranidae—pronounced "a rainy day."

You are more likely to get stung by a bee in windy weather than in any other weather condition.

Honeybees maintain a temperature of 94°F in their hives all year round.

Bees must visit some five thousand flowers to make a single spoonful of honey.

RAINING CATS AND DOGS

Dogs can suffer from tonsillitis but not appendicitis—as they don't have an appendix.

The dumbest dogs in the world are Afghan hounds.

City dogs live about three years longer than country dogs.

The world's first dog show took place in Newcastle upon Tyne in 1859 and attracted an entry of sixty pointers and setters.

A UN survey revealed that postmen in Britain are bitten by dogs far less than in any other country.

Basenji dogs and Australian dingoes are virtually identical.

The Airedale terrier was originally known as a waterside terrier.

Toy-dog breeds live an average seven years longer than large breeds.

Dogs like squeeze toys because they sound like animals in distress.

A cross between a greyhound and a terrier is a whippet.

The dog's mucus membrane is the size of fifty postage stamps.

In the United States 12,500 puppies are born every hour.

Calling a puppy to punish it teaches it not to come when it's called. It is best to reward a dog by bringing it to you—and to punish it by sending it away.

Dalmatian dogs originate from the Dalmatian coast of Croatia. Dalmatians are born pure white. Their spots don't appear until they are three or four days old.

Saint Bernard dogs do not carry kegs of brandy and never have.

The miacis, the ancestor of the dog, had retractable claws and climbed trees when it roamed the earth forty million years ago.

A normal dog has forty-two teeth: twenty in the upper jaw and twenty-two in the lower jaw. A human adult has thirty-two teeth equally divided between the two jaws.

The Jack Russell terrier was named after English church minister the Reverend John Russell.

In the United States, forty people every minute are sent to the hospital for dog bites.

Nose prints are the most reliable way of identifying dogs.

A woman who returned a book in a very tattered state to the Stroud Library in Gloucestershire, England, explained it was the fault of her dog, which had chewed it. The name of the book was *How to Train Your Dog*.

The only breed of dog that has a black, rather than a pink, tongue is a chow.

Dog food is the most profitable in the supermarket. People spend four times the amount on dog food as they do on baby food.

A cat has four rows of whiskers.

Studies show that if a cat falls off the seventh floor of a building it has about a 30 percent less chance of surviving than a cat that falls off the twentieth floor. It takes about eight floors for the cat to realize what is happening, relax, and correct itself.

The ragdoll is the largest breed of domesticated cat in the world, with adult males averaging from twenty-two to twenty-five pounds.

Cats in Halifax, Nova Scotia, Canada, have a very high probability of having six toes.

Cats have more than one hundred vocal sounds, while dogs only have about ten.

Cats have five pads on their front feet and only four on their back feet.

A cat has thirty-two muscles in each ear.

A cat's jaws cannot move sideways.

The pet ferret was domesticated more than five hundred years before the house cat.

Cat urine glows in black light.

LOST IN SPACE

Although there are an estimated ten trillion stars in our galaxy, only some three thousand of them are visible from earth with the naked eye.

Only one satellite has ever been destroyed by a meteor—the European Space Agency's Olympus in 1993.

Every year the earth becomes about twelve tons heavier because of meteorites landing.

The strongest surface winds in the solar system are found on Neptune, where they have been measured at fifteen hundred miles per hour.

When press tycoon William Randolph Hearst sent a telegram to a leading astronomer asking if there was life on Mars and to please cable a thousand words on the subject, he received the reply, "Nobody knows," repeated five hundred times.

Without an atmosphere, the surface temperature on earth at the equator would be 176°F by day and fall to –220°F at night.

The largest known mountain in the solar system is on Mars and is called Olympus Mons. It is a volcano three times the height of Everest.

A teaspoonful of neutron star material would weigh about 110 million tons.

A 150-pound adult on earth would weigh 250 tons on the sun.

On takeoff, an Apollo spacecraft develops more power than all the cars in Britain put together.

When *Voyager 2* visited Neptune, it filmed a small, irregular white triangle that zips around Neptune's surface every sixteen hours or so and is now known as the Scooter.

Each day, four and a half pounds of sunlight strike the earth.

There is now 841.6 pounds of the moon on the earth. That is the amount of rock and soil brought back by American astronauts on their six expeditions there.

Each year the moon's orbit moves about one and a half inches farther away from the earth.

If you were ejected into space, you would explode before you suffocated because there is no air pressure.

For every extra kilogram carried on a space flight, 530 kilograms of extra fuel are need at liftoff.

Any free-moving liquid will form itself into a sphere in outer space because of its surface tension.

Very tall buildings naturally lean toward the course of the sun.

If the ozone in the atmosphere were compressed to a pressure equal to that at the earth's surface, the layer would be only three millimeters thick.

The earth's atmosphere is proportionately thinner than the skin of an apple.

Venus is the only planet that rotates clockwise.

Two thousand pounds of space dust and other debris fall on the earth every day.

The moon weighs 81,000 trillion tons.

The red supergiant star Betelgeuse has a diameter larger than that of the earth's orbit around the sun—186 million miles.

MOTHER NATURE

From one giant redwood, or sequoia, it would be possible to build sixty average-sized houses. The trees can grow to over three hundred feet in height and twenty-five feet in diameter.

The growth rate of some bamboo plants can reach three feet a day.

Every part of the hemlock plant is deadly poisonous—the flowers, leaves, roots, stems, and seeds.

A fully mature oak tree sheds about seven hundred thousand leaves every year.

The name of fungal remains found in coal is sclerotinite.

Bacteria increase from one to one billion in a petri dish in twenty-four hours.

Water, which boils at 212°F at sea level, will boil at 150°F at the top of Mount Everest.

Solid hydrogen is the densest substance in the world at 70.6 grams per cubic centimeter.

Hot water is heavier than cold water.

So far, man has survived on earth for two million years. The dinosaurs lasted 150 million years.

AMAZING DISCOVERIES

An instrument developed at the University of Arizona by Dr. Frank Low for taking temperature readings of distant planets was so sensitive it was capable of detecting a lit cigarette ten thousand miles away.

A computer program named HITMAN (Homicide Information Tracking Management Automation Network) has been developed by the Los Angeles Police Department to help solve murders.

The microwave was invented after a researcher walked by a radar tube and a chocolate bar melted in his pocket.

ANATOMICALLY CORRECT

Americans use sixteen thousand tons of aspirin each year.

Banging your head against a wall burns 150 calories an hour.

The average human brain is 80 percent water.

There are at least one hundred thousand chemical

reactions going on in a normal human brain every second.

The arteries and veins surrounding the brainstem look like a stick person with the blood vessels called the Circle of Willis forming a large head.

The whole of a human's skin weighs twice as much as his brain.

The human brain stops growing at the age of eighteen.

The storage capacity of a human brain exceeds four terrabytes.

DENTAL FIGURES

The human tooth has about fifty-five miles of canals in it.

In 1977 a thirteen-year-old child found a tooth growing out of his left foot.

Gentlemen in the eighteenth century used cork pads, or plumpers, to fill out the hollows left in their cheeks by the loss of rotten teeth.

The average talker sprays about three hundred microscopic saliva drops per minute—about two and a half droplets per word.

The permanent teeth that erupt to replace the baby teeth are called succedaneous teeth.

More than thirty million people in the United States suffer from diastema—a gap between the two upper front teeth.

Societies in ancient Rome, Germany, and China used urine as a mouthwash.

Women suffer more tooth decay than men do.

We still retain some of our caveman ancestors' reactions. That is why our hair stands on end when we are frightened: it is a reaction meant to scare off our enemies by making us look taller.

A Laforte fracture is a fracture of all facial bones.

The average human bladder can hold thirteen fluid ounces of liquid.

It would be possible to boil about eight gallons of water with the heat generated by an average adult each day.

The muscle with the longest name in the human body is the *levator labii superioris alaeque nasi*—one of the muscles of facial expression acting on the mouth and nose.

The tongue is the only muscle in your body that is attached at only one end. The only bone not connected to another bone in the human body is in the throat, at the back of the tongue.

Humans are the only primates that do not have pigment in the palms of their hands.

Fingernails grow nearly four times faster than toenails.

Your right lung takes in more air than your left lung.

There are more than one hundred million light-sensitive cells in each of your retinas.

The average person inhales at about force 2 (a light breeze) on the wind-strength Beaufort scale.

A third of all cancers are sun-related.

An average adult has around 2,381,248 sweat glands on his skin.

So important to human dexterity is the thumb that the brain devotes a larger portion to controlling it than to controlling the chest and abdomen.

Lycanthropy is a disease in which a man thinks he's a wolf. *Lycanthrope* is the scientific name for "wolfman" or "werewolf."

You lose enough dead skin cells in your lifetime to fill eight five-pound flour bags.

The longest known record for constipation is 102 days.

There are forty-five miles of nerves in the human body.

The heaviest organs in the human body are the lungs, which together weigh about forty-two ounces.

If you were locked in a completely sealed room you would die of carbon dioxide poisoning before oxygen deprivation.

Your thumb is the same length as your nose.

The largest-known kidney stone weighed almost three pounds.

The most sensitive finger is the forefinger.

Surgeons perform better during operations if they are listening to music.

In a survey of eighty thousand American women it was found that those who drank moderately had only half the heart-attack risk of those who didn't drink at all.

A human mucus membrane, which is used to smell, is the size of a first-class postage stamp.

Identical twins do not have identical fingerprints.

According to a Gallup poll, 29 percent of people find the Christmas holidays more stressful than enjoyable. Nearly one in four people finds they have more headaches during the Christmas season than at any other time of year.

🌰 OH, BABY

During pregnancy, a woman's blood volume can increase by up to 50 percent to a total of twelve pints. This is in reserve against possible loss of blood during delivery.

Only 25 percent of babies are born on the day predicted by the doctor or midwife.

Sixty percent of babies are born before breakfast.

Two centuries ago, a newborn baby had less chance of surviving one week than a ninety-year-old.

According to medical experts, babies dream in the womb.

Babies are born without kneecaps. They do not appear until the child reaches two to six years of age.

You blink more than ten million times a year.

A sneeze travels out of your mouth at more than one hundred miles per hour.

It is impossible to sneeze with your eyes open.

When you sneeze, all your bodily functions stop—including the heart.

The human heart creates enough pressure to squirt blood thirty feet.

It takes only seven pounds of pressure to rip off your ear.

The spots of light you see when you rub your eyes are called phosphenes.

The white area at the base of a fingernail is called the lunula.

Skin temperature does not go much above 95°F even on the hottest day.

Thumbnails grow much more slowly than fingernails.

Your hearing becomes less sharp after eating too much.

Doctors in Florida found that patients undergoing certain operations bled twice as quickly when the moon was in its second quarter.

Your stomach has to produce a new layer of mucus every two weeks or it will digest itself.

The two most common surgeries are biopsies and Caesarean sections.

Ingrown toenails are hereditary.

The lining of your digestive system is shed every three days.

The little lump of flesh just forward of the ear canal and immediately next to the temple is called a tragus.

You burn more calories sleeping than watching television.

The skin that peels off after sunburn is called blype.

You can avoid sinking in quicksand by lying on your back and raising your legs slowly.

The average person flexes the joints in his fingers twenty-four million times in his lifetime.

There are sixty-two thousand miles of arteries, veins, and blood capillaries in the human body.

After human death, postmortem rigidity starts in the head, travels to the feet, and leaves the same way it came—head to toe.

SPLITTING HAIRS

A human hair is ten thousand times thicker than the film of a soap bubble.

Two out of every five women in the United States dye their hair.

Balding men going to hair clinics have an average age of twenty-four years and five months.

One human hair can support more than six and a half pounds.

Intelligent people have more zinc and copper in their hair.

There are 450 hairs in an average eyebrow.

Women started removing hair from their legs in 400 BCE. They either plucked them with tweezers or singed them with a flame.

TECHNOLOGICALLY ADVANCED

The first hard drive available for the Apple computer had a capacity of five megabytes.

EEG stands for electroencephalogram or electroencephalograph.

The strength of early lasers was measured in Gillettes—the number of razor blades a given beam could puncture.

Compact discs read from the inside to the outside edge—the reverse of how a record works.

There are enough explosives on earth to annihilate mankind fifty thousand times over.

The average computer user blinks seven times a minute.

When the walkie-talkie was first introduced commercially, in 1934, it was described as a "portable super-regenerative receiver and transmitter."

The first Rolls Royce, marketed in 1906, sold for about $784. Now it would fetch about $295,000.

The first Ford cars had Dodge engines.

The word *pixel* is a contraction of "picture cell" or "picture element."

The top speed of the Zamboni ice-resurfacing machine is nine miles per hour.

Scientists working on the Manhattan Project in the early 1940s measured the time it took for an imploding shell of uranium to reach critical mass and initiate spontaneous fission in "shakes of a lamb's tail." One "shake" equaled 1×10^{-8} s (one hundred millionth of a second). It took about three shakes of a lamb's tail.

In 1976 the swine flu vaccine caused more deaths than the illness it was intended to prevent.

Peanuts are one of the ingredients of dynamite.

The antibiotic nystatin, which is used chiefly to treat fungal infections such as thrush, is named after New York State, where it was developed.

The straw was developed by Egyptian brewers to taste beer without removing the fermenting ingredients that floated on the top of the container.

Holes are put in fly swatters to lower air resistance.

CRUNCHING NUMBERS

The billionth decimal digit of the numerical value pi is nine.

It took a nineteenth-century Danish schoolmaster a lifetime to calculate pi to eight hundred decimal places. It took a modern computer only a few seconds to check his figures and find them correct.

The only time in history when the roman numerals in a year were written using all the numerals in order from highest value to lowest value was 1666—MDCLXVI (1,000 plus 500 plus 100 plus 50 plus 10 plus 5 plus 1).

If you divide the Great Pyramid's perimeter by twice its height you get pi to the fifteenth digit.

One year contains 31,557,600 seconds.

An infinity sign is called a lemniscate.

In 1908 the Leaning Tower of Pisa officially weighed 14,486 tons. By 1973 it was officially slimmed to 14,200 tons.

The surface area of an average-sized brick is seventy-nine square centimeters.

ALL THAT GLITTERS

Pearls melt in vinegar.

A cubic mile of seawater contains, on average, more than $117 million worth of gold and $11 million worth of silver.

To be classified as sterling, an object must contain 92.5 percent silver.

GENDER WARS

Women's hearts beat faster than men's.

Men get hiccups more often than women do.

Women blink twice as often as men do.

WEATHER PATTERNS

Winters were colder a thousand years ago. In 1063, the River Thames froze for fourteen weeks.

After a flash of lightning, the sound of the thunder travels about a mile every five seconds. This allows you to calculate how distant the storm is.

Various types of lightning have been identified by meteorologists. The temperature of the Positive Giant type of lightning bolt reaches 54,032°F—over five times hotter than the surface of the sun.

Lightning strikes about six thousand times per minute on the earth.

It would take seven billion particles of fog to fill a teaspoon.

Raindrops are not teardrop-shaped; they are rounded at the top and flat on the bottom.

WORDS OF WISDOM

POLITICAL FIGURES

 SIR WINSTON CHURCHILL

"A lie gets halfway around the world before the truth has a chance to get its pants on."

"A pessimist sees the difficulty in every opportunity; an optimist sees the opportunity in every difficulty."

"He has all the virtues I dislike and none of the vices I admire."

"If you are going through hell, keep going."

"I am ready to meet my Maker. Whether my Maker is prepared for the great ordeal of meeting me is another matter."

"Those who survived the San Francisco earthquake said, 'Thank God I'm still alive.' But, of course,

those who died, their lives will never be the same again."
—Senator Barbara Boxer

"A billion here, a billion there, sooner or later it adds up to real money."
—Congressman Everett Dirksen

"I worship the quicksand he walks in."
—Political humorist Art Buchwald

"We're going to move left and right at the same time."
—California governor Jerry Brown

"If you take out the killings, Washington actually has a very low crime rate."
—The mayor of Washington

"That's just the tip of the ice cube."
—Tory MP Neil Hamilton, speaking on BBC2

"We are not without accomplishment. We have managed to distribute poverty equally."
—Vietnam's Foreign Minister

"Life is very important to Americans."
—Senator Bob Dole

"I've read about foreign policy and studied—I know the number of continents."
> —Presidential candidate George Wallace

"I don't like this word *bomb*. It is not a bomb but a device that is exploding."
> —French Ambassador Jacques Leblanc, speaking on
>   nuclear weapons

"The Internet is a great way to get on the 'net."
> —Senator Bob Dole

"I didn't know 'Onward Christian Soldiers' was a Christian song."
> —Texas politician Aggie Pate

"We are trying to change the 1974 Constitution, whenever that was passed."
> —Louisiana State Representative Donald Kennard

"I haven't committed a crime. All I did was fail to comply with the law."
> —New York City Mayor David Dinkins, on failing to
>   pay taxes

"I invented the Internet."
> —Vice President Al Gore

"China is a big country, inhabited by many Chinese."
> —French President Charles de Gaulle

TEXAS SPEAKER OF THE HOUSE GIB LEWIS

"I cannot tell you how grateful I am—I am filled with humidity."

"This is unparalyzed in the state's history."

"And now will you all stand and be recognized."
—Texas House Speaker Gib Lewis, to a crowd in wheelchairs on Disability Day

"There is no housing shortage in Lincoln today. Just a rumor that is put about by people who have nowhere to live."
—Mayor of Lincoln G. L. Murfin

"I favor access to discrimination on the basis of sexual orientation."
—Senator Ted Kennedy

"Whoever designed the streets must have been drunk. I think it was those Irish guys."
—Minnesota Governor Jesse Ventura

"What we have is two important values in conflict. Freedom of speech and our desire for healthy campaigns and a healthy democracy. You can't have both."
—Missouri representative Dick Gephardt

"His ignorance is encyclopedic."

— Israeli diplomat and politician Abba Eban

"The president has kept all of the promises he intended to keep."

— Clinton aide George Stephanopolous

"In America, anybody can be president. That's one of the risks you take."

— Politician and diplomat Adlai Stevenson

"It is white."

— President George W. Bush, describing the White House

"I find that the harder I work, the more luck I seem to have."

— President Thomas Jefferson

PRESIDENT BILL CLINTON

"You know the one thing that's wrong with this country? Everyone gets a chance to have their fair say."

"I'm someone who has a deep emotional attachment to *Starsky and Hutch*."

"Politics gives guys so much power that they tend to behave badly around women. And I hope I never get into that."

"The world is more like it is now than it ever was before."
—President Dwight D. Eisenhower

"I have opinions of my own, strong opinions, but I don't always agree with them."
—President George W. Bush

"If I were two-faced, would I be wearing this one?"
—President Abraham Lincoln

🔔 PRESIDENT RICHARD NIXON

"I was under medication when I made the decision to burn the tapes."

"Solutions are not the answer."

"I would have made a good Pope."

"Facts are stupid things."
—President Ronald Reagan

"I think 'Hail to the Chief' has a nice ring to it."
—President John F. Kennedy, when asked to name his favorite song

"Forgive your enemies, but never forget their names."
—President John F. Kennedy

VICE PRESIDENT DAN QUAYLE

"I love California. I practically grew up in Phoenix."

"If we don't succeed we run the risk of failure."

"It is wonderful to be here in the great state of Chicago."

"Illegitimacy is something we should talk about in terms of not having."

"It's time for the human race to enter the solar system."

"It isn't pollution that is hurting the environment, it's the impurities in our air and water that are doing it."

"What a waste it is to lose one's mind. Or not to have a mind is being very wasteful. How true that is."

"The Holocaust was an obscene period in our nation's history. I mean in this century's history. But we all lived in this century. I didn't live in this century."

"People that are really very weird can get into sensitive positions and have a tremendous impact on history."

"We are not ready for an unforeseen event that may or may not occur."

"Hawaii is a unique state. It is a state that is by itself. It is different from the other forty-nine states. Well, all states are different, but it's got a particularly unique situation."

"If you give a person a fish, they'll fish for a day. But if you train a person to fish, they'll fish for a lifetime."

ROYAL RHETORIC

"The monarchy exists, not for its own benefit, but for that of the country. We don't come here for our health. We can think of better ways of enjoying ourselves."

— Prince Philip, touring Canada

"Which are the monkeys?"

— Prince Philip, when confronted by apes and journalists in Gibraltar

"Isn't it a pity that Louis XVI was sent to the scaffold?"

— Prince Philip, to a French Minister

"I hope to God that he breaks his bloody neck."

— Prince Philip, about a press cameraman's accident

"It's a pleasant change to be in a country that isn't ruled by its people."

— Prince Philip, to Paraguay's dictator

"You have the mosquitoes, we have the press."

— Prince Philip, in the Dominican Republic

"It's the best way of wasting money that I know of."

— Prince Philip, about the American moon shot

PRINCE PHILIP

"We live above the shop."

"My only tangible contribution to British life has been to improve the rear lights on lorries."

"Tom Jones? He's made a million and he's a bloody awful singer."

"The art world thinks of me as an uncultured, polo-playing clot."

"I'm one of those stupid bums who never went to university, and it hasn't done me any harm."

"You do get fed up with being referred to like a police dog."

—Prince Charles, on the American tendency to address him simply as "Prince"

PRINCE CHARLES

"I'm one of those stupid bums who went to university. Well, I think it's helped me."

"I am often asked whether it is through some genetic trait that I stand with my hands behind my back like my father. The answer is that we both have the same tailor. He makes our sleeves so tight that we can't get our hands in front."

"Marriage is the last decision on which I would want my head to be ruled by my heart."

"My presstitutes."

—Prince Andrew, about journalists

"I have been trained in private never to show emotion in public."

—Queen Elizabeth II

THE QUEEN MOTHER

"My favorite pastime is sitting in bed eating chocolates while reading poetry."

"My favorite program is *Mrs. Dale's Diary*. I try never to miss it because it is the only way of knowing what goes on in a middle-class family."

"I don't mind praying to the eternal father, but I must be the only man in the country afflicted with an eternal mother."

—King Edward VII, about Queen Victoria

"Handsome I cannot think him, with that painfully small and narrow head, those immense features, and total want of chin. I never can or shall look at him without a shudder."

—Queen Victoria, on the future King Edward VII

"I fear the seventh granddaughter and fourteenth grandchild becomes a very uninteresting thing—for it seems to me to go on like rabbits in Windsor Park."

—Queen Victoria

"Oh, doctor, can I have no more fun in bed?"

—Queen Victoria, after her doctor's advice to have no more children

"He slept in long white drawers, which enclosed his feet as well as his legs, like the sleeping suits worn by small babies."

—Queen Victoria, on Albert's night clothes

"She ought to get a good whipping."

—Queen Victoria, about a suffragette

QUEEN ELIZABETH I

"There is only one Jesus Christ. All the rest is a dispute over trifles."

"We princes are set, as it were, upon stages in the sight and view of all the world."

"God's wounds! I will pull down my breeches and they shall also see my arse."

—King James I, when told the public wished to see him

"To make women learned and foxes tame has the same defect—to make them more cunning."

—King James I

"You can get used to anyone's face in a week."

—King Charles II, about his new bride

KING GEORGE V, TO HIS SON, THE FUTURE KING EDWARD VIII

"You dress like a cad. You act like a cad. You are a cad. Get out!"

"Never refuse an invitation to take the weight off your feet and seize every opportunity you can to relieve yourself."

"My father was frightened of his mother. I was frightened of my father. And I am damned well going to see that my children are frightened of me."

—King George V

"What did you do about peeing?"

—King George V, to Charles Lindbergh after he flew the Atlantic solo

"How would you like to make a thousand speeches and never once be allowed to say what you think yourself?"

—King Edward VIII, to Churchill

"Every drop of blood in my veins is German."
—King Edward VIII

"I did not realize I could really hate people as I do the Germans, though I never liked them."
—Queen Mary, 1941

"False, lying, cowardly, nauseous puppy. The greatest ass, liar, and beast in the world."
—King George III, on his eldest son, Prince Frederick

"I wish the ground would open up this minute and sink the monster into the lowest hole in hell."
—Queen Caroline, on her eldest son, Prince Frederick

"I shall go back to bed. I have never slept with a queen before."
—King William IV, on acceding to the throne

"Wishing myself in my sweetheart's arms, whose pretty dukkys [breasts] I trust shortly to kiss."
—King Henry VIII, in a letter to Anne Boleyn

"I am not well. Pray get me a glass of brandy."
—King George IV, in reaction to meeting his arranged bride

"It was more like being kidnapped."
—Princess Margaret, on her visit to Morocco

"You look after your empire and I will look after my life."

> —Princess Margaret, after being reproached by the Queen

"I have as much privacy as a goldfish in a bowl."

> —Princess Margaret

"A miserly martinet with an insatiable sexual appetite."

> —Prince Frederick, on his father, King George III

"This country makes me gasp—and it isn't just the altitude."

> —Princess Alexandra, on Mexico

"Being pregnant is the occupational hazard of being a wife."

> —Princess Anne

"I can't see in this bloody wind."

> —Princess Anne, age thirteen to the Queen

"He will be known for a long time because of me."

> —Duchess of Windsor, about the Duke

"A woman can never be too rich or too thin."

> —Duchess of Windsor

STAGE DIRECTIONS

"If it weren't for electricity we'd all be watching television by candlelight."

—Actor/comedian George Gobel

"Good-looking people turn me off, myself included."

—Patrick Swayze

"You'd better learn secretarial work—or else get married."

—Model agent Emmeline Strively, speaking to Marilyn Monroe in 1944

"Now there's a broad with her future behind her."

—Fellow performer Constance Bennett, describing the young Marilyn Monroe

MAE WEST

"When choosing between two evils, I always like to try the one I've never tried before."

"I used to be Snow White, but I drifted."

"He who hesitates is a damned fool."

"Domestic and foreign."

—Mae West, when asked what two types of men she preferred

"Who the hell wants to hear actors talk?"

—Warner Brothers, 1927

"It's like when I buy a horse. I don't want a thick neck and short legs."

—Mickey Rourke, on his ideal woman

"Happiness is good health and a bad memory."

—Ingrid Bergman

"If I had a choice of having a woman in my arms or shooting a bad guy on a horse, I'd take the horse. It's a lot more fun."

—Kevin Costner

"Be nice to people on your way up because you meet them on your way down."

—Jimmy Durante

"God gave men both a penis and a brain, but unfortunately not enough blood supply to run both at the same time."

—Robin Williams, commenting on the Clinton sex
scandal

"I don't want to achieve immortality through my work; I want to achieve immortality through not dying."

—Woody Allen

"Tragedy is when I cut my finger. Comedy is when you walk into an open sewer and die."

—Mel Brooks

"I don't feel we did wrong in taking this great country away from them. There were great numbers of people who needed new land, and the Indians were selfishly trying to keep it to themselves."

—John Wayne

"When I'm a blonde I can say the world is purple, and they'll believe me because they weren't listening to me."

—Kylie Bax, model and actress

"The only happy artist is a dead artist, because only then you can't change. After I die, I'll probably come back as a paintbrush."

—Sylvester Stallone

"Smoking kills. If you're killed you've lost a very important part of your life."

—Brooke Shields, during an antismoking campaign

"From the moment I picked your book up until I laid it down I was convulsed with laughter. Some day I intend reading it."

—Groucho Marx

FOOTNOTES

🌰 SOCRATES, 400 BCE

"Children today are tyrants. They contradict their parents, gobble their food, and tyrannize their teachers. I despair for the future."

"My advice to you is get married: if you find a good wife you'll be happy; if not, you'll become a philosopher."

"Maybe this world is another planet's Hell."
—Aldous Huxley

"I've just learned about his illness. Let's hope it's nothing trivial."
—Reporter and writer Irvin S. Cobb

"Fiction writing is great. You can make up almost anything."
—Ivana Trump, after her first novel was published

🌰 OSCAR WILDE

"To love oneself is the beginning of a lifelong romance."

"The only way to get rid of a temptation is to yield to it."

"There are only two tragedies in life: one is not getting what one wants, and the other is getting it."

"The covers of this book are too far apart."

—Newspaper columnist and novelist Ambrose Bierce

"Many a man's reputation would not know his character if they met on the street."

—Author Elbert Hubbard

"A period novel about the Civil War? Who needs the Civil War now? Who cares?"

—*Pictorial Review* editor when offered *Gone With the Wind* for serialization in 1936

"I'm living so far beyond my income that we may almost be said to be living apart."

—E. E. Cummings

"Everywhere I go I'm asked if I think the university stifles writers. My opinion is that they don't stifle enough of them."

—Flannery O'Connor

GEORGE BERNARD SHAW

"There are some experiences in life which should not be demanded twice from any man, and one of them is listening to the Brahms Requiem."

"If you can't get rid of the skeleton in your closet, you'd best teach it to dance."

"The longer I live the more I see that I am never wrong about anything, and that all the pains that I have so humbly taken to verify my notions have only wasted my time."

MUSIC NOTES

"We don't like their sound. Groups of guitars are on the way out."

—Decca Records, speaking about the Beatles

"Does the album have any songs you like that aren't on it?"

—Music reviewer Harry News

"If I had as many love affairs as you have given me credit for, I would now be speaking to you from a jar in the Harvard Medical School."

—Frank Sinatra, speaking to reporters

"I'd rather be dead than singing 'Satisfaction' when I'm forty-five."

—Mick Jagger

"I patterned my look after Cinderella, Mother Goose, and the local hooker."

—Dolly Parton

"I don't know anything about music. In my line you don't have to."

—Elvis Presley

"I think you can't repeat the first time of something."
—Natalie Imbruglia

"Whenever I watch TV and I see those poor starving kids all over the world, I can't help but cry. I mean I would love to be skinny like that, but not with all those flies and death and stuff."
—Mariah Carey

"Knowledge speaks, but wisdom listens."
—Jimi Hendrix

"I wish men had boobs because I like the feel of them. It's so funny, when I record I sing with a hand over each of them. Maybe it's a comfort thing."
—Emma Bunton (Baby Spice)

"Where the hell is Australia, anyway?"
—Britney Spears

"I say no to drugs. But they don't listen."
—Marilyn Manson

"Assassins!"
—Italian conductor Arturo Toscanini, speaking to his orchestra

"Listen, everyone is entitled to my opinion."
—Madonna

"Too many pieces of music finish too long after the end."

—Igor Stravinsky

MISCELLANEOUS MOUTHFULS

"You can get more with a kind word and a gun than you can with a kind word alone."

—Al Capone

"Whether you think that you can, or that you can't, you are usually right."

—Henry Ford

NAPOLEON BONAPARTE

"Never interrupt your enemy when he is making a mistake."

"Glory is fleeting, but obscurity is forever."

"My Lord, we find the man who stole the mare not guilty."

—Welsh jury foreman

"It was not my kind of people. There wasn't a producer, a press agent, a director, or an actor."

—Zsa Zsa Gabor, about her trial jury

"A man in love is incomplete until he is married. Then he is finished."
—Zsa Zsa Gabor

"Hi, I'm Dean White. Dick of the college."
—Duke University Dean Richard White

ALBERT EINSTEIN

"Reality is merely an illusion, albeit a very persistent one."

"Make everything as simple as possible, but not simpler."

"Only two things are infinite, the universe and human stupidity, and I'm not sure about the former."

"Not everything that can be counted counts, and not everything that counts can be counted."

"The true measure of a man is how he treats someone who can do him absolutely no good."
—Samuel Johnson

"I don't diet. I just don't eat as much as I'd like to."
—Linda Evangelista

"If history repeats itself I should think we can expect the same thing again."
—Terry Venables, British professional soccer player

"If you can count your money, you don't have a billion dollars."
—J. Paul Getty

"If women didn't exist, all the money in the world would have no meaning."
—Aristotle Onassis

"Whatever is begun in anger ends in shame."
—Benjamin Franklin

"We don't necessarily discriminate. We simply exclude certain types of people."
—Colonel Gerald Wellman

"The people in the navy look on motherhood as being compatible with being a woman."
—Rear Admiral James R. Hogg

"He's passé. Nobody cares about Mickey anymore. There are whole batches of Mickeys we just can't give away. I think we should phase him out!"
—Roy Disney, to brother Walt, 1937

"I love Mickey Mouse more than any woman I have ever known."
—Walt Disney

"If people get a kick out of running down pedestrians, you have to let them do it."

—Video-game director Paul Jacobs

"Models are like baseball players. We make a lot of money quickly, but all of a sudden we're thirty years old, we don't have a college education, we're qualified for nothing, and we're used to a very nice lifestyle. The best thing is to marry a movie star."

—Cindy Crawford

"The object of war is not to die for your country but to make the other bastard die for his."

—General George Patton

"I'm all in favor of keeping dangerous weapons out of the hands of fools. Let's start with typewriters."

—Frank Lloyd Wright

"I deny the allegations and I deny the alligators."

—a Chicago alderman, when indicted

"Sit by the homely girl; you'll look better by comparison."

—Debra Maffett, Miss America 1983

"If you think it was an accident, applaud."

—Journalist and talk-show host Geraldo Rivera, speaking to his TV audience on Natalie Wood's drowning

"If you haven't got anything nice to say about anybody, come sit next to me."
—Alice Roosevelt Longworth

"In the end, we will remember not the words of our enemies, but the silence of our friends."
—Martin Luther King Jr.

SAMUEL GOLDWYN

"A bachelor's life is no life for a single man."

"A verbal contract is not worth the paper it's written on."

"I was provided with additional input that was radically different from the truth. I assisted in furthering that version."
—Colonel Oliver North, testifying on Iran-Contra

"We've got to pause and ask ourselves—how much clean air do we need?"
—Ex–Chrysler Chairman Lee Iacocca

"I've always thought that underpopulated countries in Africa are vastly underpopulated."
—World Bank chief economist Lawrence Summers

"After finding no qualified candidates for the position of principal, the school board is extremely pleased to announce the appointment of David Steele to the post."

—Rhode Island Superintendent of Schools

"The streets are safe in Philadelphia. It's only the people who make them unsafe."

—Ex–Police Chief Frank Rizzo

"A friendship founded on business is better than a business founded on friendship."

—John D. Rockefeller

GIVE US A SIGN

"Permitted vehicles not allowed."

—Road sign on U.S. Highway 27

"Wonderful bargains for men with 16 and 17 necks."

—Clothing store sign

"Teeth extracted by the latest Methodists."

—Hong Kong dental ad

"Danger. Slow men at work."

—Brunei road sign

"Ladies are requested not to have children at the bar."

—Norwegian bar notice

"What does a 'No Parking' sign at a certain location mean?"

—Multiple-choice question on New York driving test

SPORTING FIGURES

"The word *genius* isn't applicable in football. A genius is a guy like Norman Einstein."

—Sports analyst Joe Theisman

"We talked five times. He called me twice and I called him twice."

—California Angels coach

"These people haven't seen the last of my face. If I go down, I'm going down standing up."

—Basketball player Chuck Person

"I have a God-given talent. I got it from my dad."

—Missouri sportsman Julian Wakefield

"I may be dumb but I'm not stupid."

—Football announcer Terry Bradshaw

🏈 BASEBALL MANAGER CASEY STENGEL

"If you walk backward, you'll find out that you can go forward and people won't know if you're coming or going."

"The team has come along slow but fast."

"In a sense, it's a one-man show. Except there are two men involved."

—John Motson, BBC sports commentator

"Pitching is 80 percent of the game. The other half is hitting and fielding."

—Baseball player Mickey Rivers

"Sometimes they write what I say and not what I mean."

—Baseball player Pedro Guerrero, about the press

"We didn't lose. We weren't beaten. We just came in second."

—Commentator at the 1996 Olympics

"I've never had major knee surgery on any other part of my body."

—Basketball player Winston Bennet

"The doctors X-rayed my head and found nothing."

—Baseball player Dizzy Dean

BASEBALL PLAYER YOGI BERRA

"I really didn't say everything I said."

"Always go to other people's funerals, otherwise they won't go to yours."

"It's like déjà vu all over again."

"Predictions are difficult, especially about the future."

"A nickel ain't worth a dime anymore."

"You got to be careful if you don't know where you're going, because you might not get there."

"Sure there have been injuries and deaths in boxing, but none of them serious."
—Boxer Alan Minter

"My sister's expecting a baby, and I don't know if I'm going to be an uncle or an aunt."
—Basketball player Chuck Nevitt

"Our strength is we don't have any weaknesses. Our weakness is that we don't have any real strengths."
—College football coach Frank Broyles

"He's a guy who gets up at six o'clock in the morning regardless of what time it is."
—Boxing trainer Lou Duva

"Any time Detroit scores more than one hundred points and holds the other team below one hundred points they almost always win."
—Basketball commentator Doug Collins

"The places where I need work are on my inside and outside games."

—Basketball player Darnell Hillman

"Sonny Liston has a very unusual injury, a dislocated soldier."

—Boxer Henry Cooper, on the BBC

SPORTS COMMENTATOR MURRAY WALKER

"Except for his car he's the only man on the track."

"The lead car is absolutely unique, except for the one behind it, which is identical."

"He treats us like men. He lets us wear earrings."

—Houston sportsman Tonin Polk

"Next up is the Central African Republic, located in Central Africa."

—Sports commentator Bob Costas

"Morcelli has four fastest 1,500-meter times ever. And all those times are at 1,500 meters."

—Sports commentator David Coleman

"If everything seems under control, you're just not going fast enough."

—Grand Prix legend Mario Andretti

"Strangely, in slow-motion replay, the ball seemed to hang in the air for even longer."
—Sports commentator David Acfield

"We're just physically not physical enough."
—Basketball coach Denny Crum

"I owe a lot to my parents, especially my mother and father."
—Golfer Greg Norman

FLORIDA STATE FOOTBALL COACH BILL PETERSON

"You guys pair up in groups of three, then line up in a circle."

"Men, I want you just thinking of one word all season. One word and one word only: Super Bowl."

"You guys have to run a little more than full speed out there."

"You guys line up alphabetically by height."

"If only faces could talk."
—Sportscaster Pat Summerall

"He's been around for a while and he's pretty old.

He's thirty-five years old. That will give you some idea of how old he is."

—Broadcaster Ron Fairley

"What will you do when you leave football, Jack? Will you stay in football?"

—Stuart Hall, BBC Radio 5

"We all get heavier as we get older because there's a lot more information in our heads."

—Basketball player Vlade Divac

"Better make it six, I can't eat eight."

—Baseball player Dan Osinski, when asked how many slices he wanted his pizza cut into

MEDIA MENTIONS

"Outside consultants sought for test of gas chamber."

—*Arizona Republic* ad

"Most lies about blondes are false."

—*Cincinnati Times-Star*

"The Supreme Court rules that murderers shall not be electrocuted twice for the same crime."

—*Cleveland Daily News* headline

"Most hotels are already booked solid by people, plus five thousand journalists."

—*Bangkok Post*

"And now the sequence of events in no particular order."

—Dan Rather

"Weather forecast: Precipitation in the morning, rain in the afternoon."

—*Detroit Daily News*

"Most cars on our roads have only one occupant, usually the driver."

—Carol Malia, BBC TV presenter

"And as Mansell comes into the pits, he's quite literally sweating his eyeballs out."

—British TV commentator

"We are unable to announce the weather. We depend on weather reports from the airport, which is closed, due to weather. Whether we will be able to give you a weather report tomorrow will depend on the weather."

—Arab news report

"Lack of brains hinders research."

—*The Columbus Dispatch*

"During the scrimmage, Tarkanian paced the sideline with his hands in his pockets while biting his nails."
—Associated Press report

"The Queen's [Victoria's] bosom has been deliciously handled and has been brought out by the artist in full rotundity."
—*The London Times* art critic

"If you, or any member of your family, has been killed, then call us."
—Orlando lawyer's TV commercial

"Traffic is very heavy at the moment, so if you are thinking of leaving now, you'd better set off a few minutes earlier."
—Dublin radio reporter

"Man thought hurt but slightly dead."
—*The Providence Journal*

"The efforts elicited the approbation of the Royal circle."
—Victorian court circular—it meant there was applause

"Man shoots neighbor with machete."
—*The Miami Herald*

"Sure it's going to kill a lot of people, but they may be dying of something else anyway."
　　—Othal Brand, Texas pesticide review board, on
　　　chlordane

"Everything that can be invented has been invented."
　　—U.S. Patent Office, 1899

"Passive activity income does not include the following income for an activity that is not a passive activity."
　　—U.S. Internal Revenue Service form

CREATIVITY CORNER

BOOKWORMS

The first person who referred to a coward as a chicken was William Shakespeare.

The character of Hamlet has the longest of Shakespeare's speaking parts with 1,530 lines. The second longest is that of Richard III with 1,164 lines.

The only mention of the United States of America by Shakespeare was in his play *The Comedy of Errors*.

Shakespeare's daughters were called Susanna and Judith.

The father of Geoffrey Chaucer, who wrote *The Canterbury Tales*, was a London wine merchant.

In *Gone With the Wind*, Melanie's pregnancy lasts twenty-one months based on the actual battles mentioned.

James Joyce chose the date on which his novel *Ulysses* takes place in Dublin—June 16, 1904—after the day on which he had his first date with his future wife, Nora Barnacle.

Author Ian Fleming gave the name James Bond to his spy hero after seeing it on the cover of a book of West Indian birds, by ornithologist James Bond. Ian Fleming's favorite cocktail was Pink Gin and not a Vodka Martini.

Jules Verne, who wrote about amazing voyages to the moon and around the earth, only ever went aloft in a machine once—a balloon ascent in 1873.

A book published in 1940 contained 370 proofs of the Pythagorean Theorem, including one by former President James Garfield.

Alexandra Dumas named his palatial home in Paris "Monte Cristo" after his most famous novel, *The Count of Monte Cristo*.

Agatha Christie claimed she did most of the plotting for her detective stories while sitting in a bathtub eating apples.

During World War I Agatha Christie worked in a hospital dispensary, and it was there she acquired her extensive knowledge of poisons.

Pulitzer Prize–winner William Faulkner once worked as a rum runner to make money because he couldn't find a publisher to publish his novels.

John Le Carré's real name is David John Moore Cornwell.

Elizabeth Barrett Browning's pet cocker spaniel was named Flush.

Dylan Thomas once unkindly pointed out that, except for one misplaced letter, T. S. Eliot's name spelled backward is "toilets."

The Declaration of Independence was written on hemp paper.

The first name of Jeeves, the fictional butler created by P. G. Wodehouse in 1915, remained a mystery for many years (even to his employer). It was later revealed in her 1971 novel *Much Obliged Jeeves*. His name was Reginald.

One edition of the current Sunday *New York Times* has more information in it than a typical adult was exposed to in an entire lifetime a hundred years ago.

The only novel to top the bestsellers' list for two consecutive years—1972 and 1973—was Richard Bach's *Jonathan Livingston Seagull.*

Ezra Pound, William Joyce, and P. G. Wodehouse all made broadcasts for the enemy during World War II.

In 1900, Americans voted their favorite book, after the Bible, as *The Sears Roebuck Catalogue.*

Charles Dickens penned in Puny Pete, Little Larry, and Small Sam before settling on Tiny Tim for his crippled child in *A Christmas Carol.*

Charles Dickens took just six weeks to write *A Christmas Carol.*

There are twenty different kinds of kisses described in the erotic Indian text the *Kama Sutra.*

The writer Edgar Allen Poe and singer Jerry Lee Lewis both married their thirteen-year-old cousins.

Edgar Allen Poe was expelled from West Point Military Academy for turning out for a public parade wearing only his white belt and gloves.

The children's poem *The Pied Piper of Hamlyn* was written by Robert Browning.

The initials in J.R.R. Tolkien's name stand for John Ronald Reuel.

Virginia Woolf wrote all her books standing up.

The longest sentence in literature was written by Victor Hugo in *Les Misérables* and came to a staggering 823 words.

In the Batman stories the Riddler's real name was Edward Nigma or E. Nigma.

Oscar Wilde lived out the last three years of his life in France as Sebastian Melmoth.

Ernest Hemingway once admitted that he had revised the last page of *A Farewell to Arms* thirty-nine times.

According to Ernest Hemingway, four achievements are necessary to become a real man. You should plant a tree, fight a bull, write a book, and have a son.

The next-door neighbors of Miss Marple in St. Mary Mead village were Dr. Haydock and Miss Harnell.

Casanova named 116 lovers in his memoir, *The Story of my Life*, even though he often boasted of seducing thousands.

John Steinbeck worked as a hod carrier, conveying concrete along scaffolding during the construction of New York's Madison Square Garden in the 1930s.

Mick Jagger turned down a £3.5 million advance offer on his memoirs from a publisher because, he said, he "couldn't remember" enough significant details from his own life.

Robinson Crusoe was marooned on his desert island for twenty-four years.

Robin Hood's friend Little John was really named John Little.

The first names of Dr. Jekyll and Mr. Hyde were Henry and Edward.

Dr. Frankenstein's first name was Victor.

Rip Van Winkle's dog was called Victor.

ELEMENTARY, MY DEAR

Sherlock Holmes was known as Sherringford Holmes in the first short story written by Sir Arthur Conan Doyle in

1886. His sidekick was then called Ormond Sacker, who would later evolve into Thomas Watson.

Sir Arthur Conan Doyle was paid £25 for his first published story about Sherlock Holmes, *A Study in Scarlet*, which appeared in Beeton's Christmas Annual in 1887.

Dr. Watson's bullet wound moved according to different Sherlock Holmes stories. In *A Study in Scarlet* it was in his shoulder but in *The Sign of Four* it was in his leg.

Only two of the Sherlock Holmes stories are written with him as the narrator. They are *The Blanched Soldier* and *The Lion's Mane*.

Arthur Conan Doyle was awarded a knighthood for his defense of the British concentration camps during the Boer Wars and not because of his Sherlock Holmes stories.

MISSISSIPPI MAN

The first book manuscript to be typed before being sent to a publisher was Mark Twain's *The Adventures of Tom Sawyer* in 1876—when the first typewriter was manufactured.

Mark Twain failed to graduate from elementary school.

Halley's Comet came into view in 1835 when Mark Twain was born, and was again in view in 1910 when he died.

ARTISTS' COLONY

Madrid's Prado Art Museum is named after the fields that once surrounded it. Meadow, in Spanish, is *prado*.

In artist Emanuel Leutze's famous 1851 painting *Washington Crossing the Delaware* he used the Rhine in his native Germany as his model.

When asked to name his favorite among all his paintings, Pablo Picasso replied, "the next one."

Painter Jocopo Robusti became far better known by his nickname, "Little Dyer" or "Tintorette." His father was a silk dyer.

Salvador Dali's wife was the model for the Christ figure in Dali's painting *The Sacrament of the Last Supper*.

The sitter in Leonardo da Vinci's *Mona Lisa* has no eyebrows.

Each of the sunflowers in Vincent Van Gogh's painting *Sunflowers*, which sold at auction in 1987, was worth $2.66 million. There are fifteen in the painting.

Rembrandt's last name was van Ryn.

TALL TALES

Disney cleaned up the story of *Snow White and the Seven Dwarfs* for his feature cartoon. In the original Grimm Brothers fairytale the queen was condemned to dance in red-hot iron shoes until she died. Disney had her falling off a precipice to her death.

There was room for 150 knights around King Arthur's famous round table.

The Nepalese word for the Abominable Snowman is *Metohkangmi*, which means "the indescribably filthy man of the snow."

In Victorian times Goldilocks, of Three Bears fame, was known as Silver Hair. She later became Golden Hair and eventually Goldilocks.

In Africa the house of the wicked witch in *Hansel and Gretel* is not made of gingerbread but of salt—which was highly prized by children.

WORDPLAY

"Able was I ere I saw Elba" is a palindrome written by Napoleon.

"Hypersonic" means five times the speed of sound.

When a speaker accidentally transposes the initial sounds or letters of two or more words, often to humorous effect, it is called a spoonerism. For example, saying Jag of Flapan instead of Flag of Japan.

For a short time in 1967 the American Typers' Association made a new punctuation mark called an interrobang, which was a combination of the question mark and an exclamation mark. It was rarely used and hasn't been seen since.

Gambrinous is a word meaning "being full of beer."

Author Lewis Carroll combined the words *chuckle* and *snort* to come up with the word *chortle* in *Through the Looking Glass*.

Transurphobia is the fear of haircuts.

The slow-witted character named Moron in Molière's play *La Princesse d'Elide* created a new word in the dictionary.

Pasta vermicelli means "little worms."

The letter *w* is the only letter in the alphabet that does not have just one syllable. It has three.

The term *maverick* came from Texas rancher Sam Maverick, who refused to brand his calves.

The line "Three quarks for Muster Mark!" in James Joyce's *Ulysses* provided the name for the subatomic particles now known as "quarks," named by physicist Murray Gell-Mann.

The *y* in old words like *ye* is better pronounced with a *th* sound and not a *y* sound. In Latin, the *th* sound did not exist and the Romans occupying England used the rune *thorne* to represent the *th* sounds. When the printing presses were invented, the character from the Roman alphabet that most closely resembled the *thorne* was the lower case *y*.

The highest-scoring three-letter word in Scrabble is *zax*, which is a tool for cutting and trimming roof slates.

The letters of the word *SHAZAM*, which was shouted to conjure up comic-book hero Captain Marvel, stood for Solomon's Wisdom, Hercules's Strength, Atlas's Stamina, Zeus's Power, Achilles's Courage, and Mercury's Speed.

A trilemma is a dilemma with a third alternative.

The single dot over the lower-case letter *i* is called a tipple.

The most commonly used word in English conversation is *I*.

The only word in the English language that both begins and ends with the letters *und* is *underground*.

One seven-letter word that contains ten other words without any of the letters being rearranged is *therein*. It includes *the*, *there*, *he*, *in*, *rein*, *her*, *here*, *ere*, *therein*, and *herein*.

In most of the world's languages the word for mother begins with the letter *m*.

During World War II there were two types of dirigibles—the A-rigid and the B-limp. The second became the common-usage name for a dirigible—blimp.

The only Dutch word to contain eight consecutive consonants is *angstschreeuw*, meaning "cry of fear."

The English syllable *ough* can be pronounced nine different ways. One sentence that contains them all is: "A rough-coated, dough-faced thoughtful ploughman strode through the streets of Scarborough and after falling into his slough he coughed and hiccoughed."

Left-handed people cannot write Mandarin Chinese.

Dreamt is the only English word that ends in the letters *mt*.

The letters *HIOX* in the Roman alphabet are the only ones that look the same if you turn them upside down or see them from behind.

In ancient Greece, writing had no space between the words.

The shortest French word with all five vowels is *oiseau*, meaning bird.

The term *strike* originated in 1768 when British sailors refused to work and showed this by striking, or lowering, the sails on their ships.

The word *monosyllable* has five syllables.

A vexillologist studies flags.

The Australian slang term *hooloo* means "good-bye."

The Japanese word *judo* means "the gentle way."

The original meaning of the word *clue* was a ball of thread or yarn. Like its modern namesake, it often took some time to unravel.

Medieval ecclesiastical calendars had the important saints and feast days highlighted in red ink. These memorable days became known as "red-letter days."

An American billion is one thousand million—a British billion is one million million.

The full medical description of a black eye is "bilateral perorbital haematoma."

Queuetopia was a word invented by Winston Churchill to describe communist countries where people had to line up to buy anything.

A nineteenth-century advertisement for a McCoy sewing machine introduced the phrase "The real McCoy" into the English language.

Eosophobia is a fear of dawn.

The word *spam* is an acronym formed from SPiced hAM.

A duffle bag is so called because the thick wool originally used to make the bags came from the Belgium town of Duffel.

The word *robot* comes from the Czechoslovakian word *robotovat*, which means "to work very hard." It was created by Karel Capek.

The phrase "passing the buck" comes from the old American custom of using a buckhorn-handled knife, placed in front of the dealer during a game of cards. A player who didn't want the deal would pass the knife, or buckhorn, to the next player.

The difference between a nook and a cranny is that the nook is a corner and the cranny is a crack.

The State Department refers to elevators as "vertical transportation units."

In the native Greek, *Utopia* means "not a place" or "nowhere."

Race car is a palindrome.

NOTABLE QUOTABLES

Oscar Wilde once remarked that, "America was often discovered before Columbus, but it was always hushed up."

In the cartoon strip *Blondie* Dagwood once re-marked, "The trouble with the rat race is that there is never a finish line."

The phrase "United we stand, divided we fall" was first used in the Aesop fable *The Four Oxen and the Lion*, written nearly six hundred years before Christ.

It was critic, author, and poet Dorothy Parker who wrote "Men don't make passes at girls who wear glasses."

PEOPLE POINTERS

CHIEF FACTORS

Eight of America's presidents were born British subjects.

When George Washington was president there were only some 350 federal employees.

Abraham Lincoln was the only president to be awarded a patent—for a device to lift boats over shoals without discharging their cargoes.

James Madison was the smallest president in U.S. history, measuring just five feet four inches and weighing about 98 pounds.

For religious reasons Franklin Pierce was the only president to say, "I promise" instead of "I swear" at his inauguration.

Richard Milhous Nixon's name contains all the letters from the word *criminal*. He was the first U.S. president to have this distinction. The second was William Jefferson Clinton.

Every American president since World War II who addressed the Canadian House of Commons during his first term of office went on to be re-elected for a second term—Eisenhower, Nixon, Reagan, and Clinton. Kennedy, Johnson, Ford, Carter, and the first Bush, who did not address the Parliament, did not win a second term.

In the eight-year period Ronald Reagan was president, the White House bought twelve tons of his favorite jelly beans.

The only president to be head of a labor union was Ronald Reagan.

Ronald Reagan was the oldest man to be elected president of the United States.

LYNDON LINGO

Fresca, a grapefruit-flavored soda sold on the East Coast, was liked so much by Lyndon Johnson that he had a fountain installed in the Oval Office that dispensed the drink. He operated the soda fountain by pushing a button on his desk chair.

Lyndon Johnson had an aunt named Frank.

Lyndon Johnson was obsessed with secrecy. He usually wrote "burn this," even on his personal mail.

Lyndon Johnson's family all shared the initials L.B.J. They were: Lyndon Baines Johnson, Lady Bird Johnson, Linda Bird Johnson, and Lucy Baines Johnson. His dog was Little Beagle Johnson.

Jimmy Carter was the first U.S. president to have been born in a hospital.

Gerald Ford was once a male model.

Two presidential families had their own way of preventing their conversations being overheard by White House guests or staff. The Hoovers spoke to each other in Chinese. The Coolidge family spoke in sign language.

For over forty years, Herbert Hoover gave all his political earnings to charity, including his wages and pension as president.

The first president to ride in an automobile was William McKinley, after he was shot. He was taken to the hospital in a 1901 Columbia electric ambulance.

Wartime president Franklin D. Roosevelt was the first to have a presidential aircraft. He only flew on the specially equipped Douglas DC4, nick-named "the sacred cow," once—to travel to Yalta for the conference with Stalin and Churchill. The plane was fitted with a lift so he could board it in his wheelchair.

Theodore Roosevelt was the only president not to use the word *I* in his inaugural address.

Sarah Delano Roosevelt never learned to entrust her son with the management of the family's financial affairs and never thought he was up to the task—even though Franklin D. presided over eight annual budgets of the largest fiscal entity on earth: the United States.

Teddy Roosevelt was so keen on boxing he had a boxing ring installed in the White House.

During the eleven-month-long African hunting expedition that followed Theodore Roosevelt's term as president in 1909, he shot 296 animals, including nine lions and five elephants.

ANNALS OF HISTORY

The only woman in history to have married both a king of France and a king of England was Eleanor of

Aquitane. Her husbands were Louis VII of France and Henry II of England.

The "new" bridal extra, which Wallis Simpson wore to her wedding with Edward VIII, was a gold coin, which she carried in her left shoe. It had been minted for Edward's coronation.

The first English royal to wear a pair of silk stockings was a man—King Henry VIII, in 1509. The stockings were a gift from Spain.

Queen Anne's bowlegs inspired a furniture style.

Queen Victoria had a sprig of holly placed below her collar as a child to train her to keep her chin up.

The prince of Wales, later to become Edward VIII, was saved from arrest during a police Prohibition raid by singer Texas Guinan, who pushed him into her nightclub kitchen and gave him a chef's hat and skillet.

England's King Henry VI was only nine months old when he acceded to the throne.

King Louis XIV of France reigned for seventy-two years. He acceded to the throne at the age of five in 1643. He once declared: "L'Etat? C'est moi"—I am the State.

In his various palaces, King Louis XIV of France had 413 beds.

King Louis XIV of France took only three baths during his seventy-seven-year lifetime: one when he was baptized; one at the insistence of one of his mistresses; and the last when a doctor lanced a boil on his bottom and ordered him to soak it in a tub of hot water.

The last Ranee of Sarawak, who selected mistresses for her husband, the Raja, boasted that he had only ever rejected one of her choices.

Attila the Hun died of a nosebleed on his wedding night in AD 453.

William Wrigley gave away free packs of chewing gum to customers who bought his baking powder. He soon abandoned the baking powder when he discovered they were buying it in order to get his gum.

The world's first popular elected female head of state was Sirimauo Bandranaike of Sri Lanka, in 1960.

Stalin, whose left arm was noticeably shorter than his right, also had webbed toes on his left foot.

Confucius was the eleventh child of a seventy-year-old soldier.

Lee Harvey Oswald was dyslexic.

Picasso's full name was Pablo Diego Jose Francisco de Paula Juan Nepomuceno Maria de los Remedios Cipriano de la Santisima Trinidad Ruiz Picasso.

Of the 102 people on board the *Mayflower*, thirteen of them were called John.

Somdetch Thra Paramendr Naha Mongkut was otherwise known as the king of Siam—the *King and I* immortalized by writer Margaret Langden.

King Prajadhipok, the ruler of Siam, took out insurance with French and British insurance companies against unemployment. He collected and lived comfortably on the proceeds in England for six years, after which time he was overthrown in the early 1930s.

Before he discovered his real vocation as a lover and libertine, Casanova was preparing for the priesthood.

When asked what he thought of Western civilization, Mahatma Gandhi replied, "I think it would be a good idea."

The Roman emperor Nero, whose father was dead and mother in exile, was brought up by a barber and a male ballet dancer.

Stalin's real name was Iosif Vissarionovich Dzhugashvili. He began using the pseudonym *Stalin*, meaning "Man of Steel," in 1936.

Helen of Troy was queen of Sparta.

After Egypt's King Farouk was overthrown by Gamal Nasser, he predicted that one day there would be only five kings left in the world—the kings of hearts, spades, diamonds, clubs, and England.

Captain William Bligh, of *Mutiny on the Bounty* fame, was thrown out after another mutiny almost twenty years after that event. While he was governor of New South Wales, in 1808, British army officers captured him and forced him to resign. He had tried to stop the colony's rum trade.

In 1946, to celebrate Aga Khan's sixty years as leader of the Ismaili Sect of the Shiite Muslims, his followers gave him his weight in diamonds. He weighed 243 ¼ pounds.

Before founding the Russian communist party and becoming premier of the first Soviet government, Lenin lived in exile in England, under the name of Jacob Richter.

QUEEN OF THE NILE

Cleopatra used squeezed pomegranate seeds for lipstick.

Cleopatra was only twelve years old when she took her first lover.

There were six rulers of Egypt named Cleopatra before the woman who became linked with Julius Caesar and Mark Antony.

Every night Cleopatra had her mattress stuffed with rose petals.

FAMOUS BEST FRIENDS

President Andrew Jackson's pet parrot had to be removed from his funeral in 1845 because it was swearing.

Sir Walter Raleigh had a black greyhound called Hamlet.

President Lyndon Johnson called his pet beagles Him and Her. President Franklin D. Roosevelt and his wife, Eleanor, called their pistols, which they kept under their pillows, His and Hers.

George Washington named his three foxhounds Drunkard, Tippler, and Tipsy.

Polar explorer Admiral Byrd's dog was called Igloo.

The dog that shared the bed of Napoleon and Josephine was called Fortune.

Houdini actually trained his pet dog to escape from a miniature set of handcuffs.

CONTEMPORARY CHARACTERS

To thank actor Harrison Ford for narrating a documentary, the London Museum of Natural History named a spider after him called *Calponia Harrisonfordi*.

Neil Armstrong stepped onto the moon using his left foot first.

More than two hundred people in West Virginia returned their license plates to the Motor Vehicle Bureau because they began with the letters *OJ*.

The car-making Dodge brothers, Horace and John, were Jewish, which is why the first Dodge emblem had a Star of David on it.

Actor Laurence Oliver—later Lord Olivier—once

called a press conference just to complain about service on British Rail. He was furious that kippers had been dropped from the menu.

Henry Ford never had a driving license.

TALES OF THE EVERYMAN

The world's tallest woman, Zeng Jinlian, from China, was eight feet one and three-fourths inches tall. The world's tallest man was an American, Robert Wadlo, who was eight feet eleven inches tall.

The Scottish name *Campbell* actually means "crooked mouth" in Gaelic.

To celebrate his seven hundredth parachute jump, Flight Sergeant Hector Macmillan made his descent in full national Scottish dress while playing "The Road to the Isles" on the bagpipes.

More people play the bagpipes today than at any time in history.

Fleet commanders in the Pacific Theater of war in World War II, Admiral Isoroku Yamamoto for the Japanese, and Admiral Chester Nimitz for the United States, were each missing two fingers as a result of accidents while young officers on board ships.

Some American Indians did not eat turkey meat because they believed killing such a timid bird showed laziness.

There are more psychoanalysts in Buenos Aires, Argentina, than in any other city in the world.

A survey of career women who had tattoos revealed that they preferred to adorn their left breast rather than their right breast by a ratio of three to one.

Until nearly a hundred years ago almost all people in Martha's Vineyard—a resort island off the coast of Massachusetts, to the south of Cape Cod—were bilingual in sign language and English. It developed its own dialect of sign language when a deaf person arrived in 1692. Between then and 1910 the relatively large, genetically deaf population, and most other inhabitants, recognized and could use their own particular sign language.

Because snow is relatively unknown on the continent of Africa, children there know the fairy-tale heroine as "Flower White" rather than as Snow White.

By law, every Swiss citizen is required to have a bomb shelter or access to a bomb shelter.

Violet Gibson Burns typed continuously at her typewriter for 264 hours—a world record.

English haberdasher James Hetherington was arrested in 1797 when he wore a silk top hat for the first time in London. The charge read that he was guilty of wearing a "tall structure of shining lustre calculated to disturb the people."

The Irish baron of Kinsale has the privilege of retaining his hat in the presence of royalty.

In the early days of Hollywood, Western sets were made to seven-eighths scale to make the heroes seem larger.

SEVEN UP

THE MAGNIFICENT SEVEN

Charles Bronson—Bernordo
Yul Brynner—Chris
Horst Buchholz—Chico
James Coburn—Britt
Brad Dexter—Harry
Steve McQueen—Vin
Robert Vaughn—Lee

THE SEVEN DWARFS

Bashful
Doc
Dopey
Grumpy
Happy
Sleepy
Sneezy

THE SEVEN DEADLY SINS

Avarice
Envy
Gluttony
Lust
Pride
Sloth
Wrath

THE SEVEN WONDERS OF THE ANCIENT WORLD

Great Pyramid of Giza
Hanging Gardens of Babylon
Mausoleum of Halicarnassus
Temple of Artemis at Ephesus
Colossus of Rhodes
Pharos (Lighthouse) of Alexandria
Statue of Zeus at Olympia

THE SEVEN VIRTUES

Justice
Fortitude
Prudence
Temperance
Faith
Hope
Charity

THE SEVEN SEAS

North Atlantic Ocean
South Atlantic Ocean
North Pacific Ocean
South Pacific Ocean
Indian Ocean
Arctic Ocean
Antarctic Ocean

THE SEVEN SIZES OF GRAND PIANO

Baby Grand—five feet, eight inches
Living Room Grand—five feet, ten inches
Professional Grand—six feet
Drawing Room Grand—6 feet, four inches
Parlor Grand—6 feet, eight inches
Half Concert Grand—seven feet, four inches
Concert Grand—eight feet, eleven inches or
    longer

THE SEVEN CHILDREN OF BARON VON TRAPP OF THE SOUND OF MUSIC FAME

Liesel
Friedrich
Louisa

Brigitta
Kurt
Marta
Gretl

THE SEVEN COLORS OF
THE RAINBOW

Red
Orange
Yellow
Green
Blue
Indigo
Violet

THE SEVEN DAYS OF CREATION

Created heaven and earth; day and night.
Divided heaven from earth.
Created the land, the sea, and vegetation.
Created the sun, the moon, and the stars.
Created creatures great and small.
Created mankind.
Sanctified the seventh day as the day of rest.

THE SEVEN HILLS OF ROME

Palatine

Capitoline

Quirinal

Viminal

Esquiline

Caelian

Aventine

THE SEVEN AGES OF MAN
(ACCORDING TO SHAKESPEARE)

The Infant

The Schoolboy

The Lover

The Soldier

The Justice

The Pantaloon

The Second Childhood

THE SEVEN JAPANESE GODS
OF LUCK

Bishamon

Daikoku

Ebisu

Fukurokuju

Jurojin

Hotei
Benten

THE SEVEN DESTINATIONS OF THE CROSBY AND HOPE ON-THE-ROAD MOVIES (1940 TO 1962)

Rio
Hong Kong
Singapore
Zanzibar
Morocco
Utopia
Bali

THE SEVEN IONIAN ISLANDS

Corfu
Cephalonia
Zacynthus
Leucas
Ithaca
Cythera
Paxos

THE SEVEN MEDIEVAL
CHAMPIONS OF CHRISTENDOM

St. George—England

St. Denis—France

St. James—Spain

St. Anthony—Italy

St. Andrew—Scotland

St. Patrick—Ireland

St. David—Wales

THE SEVEN GIFTS OF
THE HOLY SPIRIT

Wisdom

Understanding

Counsel

Fortitude

Knowledge

Piety

Fear of the Lord

THE SEVEN SISTERS

The seven stars in the Taurus constellation visible to the naked eye, named after the daughters of the Titan Atlas and the Oceanid Pleione in Greek mythology.

Alcyone

Maia

Electra

Merope

Taygete

Celaeno

Asterope

THE SEVEN SPIRITUAL WORKS OF MERCY

To convert the sinner.

To instruct the ignorant.

To counsel those in doubt.

To comfort those in sorrow.

To bear wrongs patiently.

To forgive injuries.

To pray for the living and the dead.

THE SEVEN CORPORAL WORKS OF MERCY

To tend the sick.

To feed the hungry.

To give drink to the thirsty.

To clothe the naked.

To harbor the stranger.

To minister to prisoners.

To bury the dead.

SEEING THE WORLD

LANGUAGE BARRIERS

Rock English, a mixture of Spanish and English, is the local language spoken in Gibraltar.

In New Guinea more than seven hundred different native languages are spoken—which is a third of the world's known languages.

The political divisions of Japan are called "prefectures," whereas those of Switzerland are called "cantons."

Ethiopia means "the land of sunburned faces" in Greek.

The six official languages of the United Nations are English, French, Arabic, Chinese, Russian, and Spanish.

Nullarbor Plain in southwest Australia gets its name from the Latin *nullus arbor*—"no tree."

South Africa used to have two official languages. Now it has eleven.

Swahili is a combination of Arabic, Portuguese, and African tribal languages.

Seoul, the South Korean capital, means "capital" in the Korean language.

The word for "name" in Japanese is *na-ma-e*. In Mongolian it is *nameg*.

Louisiana's counties are actually called parishes—for example, Jefferson David Parish.

Canada is an Iroquoian Indian word meaning "big village."

Vang is the most common surname among the Hmong people of Laos.

AIN'T NO RIVER WIDE ENOUGH . . .

The Red Sea is so named after the algae, which, when dying, turns the Red Sea's normally intense blue-green waters to red.

Lake Nicaragua in Nicaragua has the only fresh-water sharks in the world.

Britain's shortest river is the Brun, which runs through Burnley in Lancashire.

The only river to flow both north and south of the equator is the Congo River, which crosses the equator twice.

Mexico's east coast is sinking into the sea at the rate of one or two centimeters a year.

On Gilbert and Ellice Islands, Britain's largest colonial territory in the Pacific, the highest point above sea level is eleven feet.

The driest place on earth is a series of valleys near Ross Island in Antarctica, where for at least the last two million years no rain has fallen.

Devon is the only county in Great Britain to have two coasts.

About one-tenth of the world's surface is permanently covered in ice.

The smallest and shallowest ocean in the world is the Arctic Ocean.

The Hudson River, running alongside Manhattan, can run in either direction depending on the tide.

At latitude 60° south you can sail all the way around the world.

Lake Baikal, in southern Siberia, is the deepest lake in the world. It was formed twenty-five to thirty million years ago and is 5,718 feet deep.

The town of Tidikelt, in the Sahara desert, went ten years without rainfall.

If you stand with your eyes about six feet above the surface of the ocean, the horizon will be about three miles away.

The record for the most snowfall in one day was set on February 7, 1916, in Alaska when seventy-eight inches fell.

In 1929, Toronto, Ontario, became home to the biggest swimming pool in the world. The pool held two thousand people and measured three hundred by seventy-five feet. It is still in operation.

The largest landlocked country in the world is Mongolia.

Ninety percent of the world's ice is contained in the Antarctic ice sheet.

The Niagara Falls have eaten their way seven miles upstream since their formation ten thousand years ago. If erosion continues at this rate they will disappear into Lake Erie in twenty-two thousand years.

Niagara Falls stopped flowing for thirty hours on March 29, 1848, because of an ice jam blocking the Niagara River.

The highest wave ever recorded—towering a full ten-stories high—was 112 feet high and seen in the North Pacific in 1933.

Birmingham, England, has more miles of canal than Venice.

Ninety-nine percent of the buildings in Reykjavik, the capital of Iceland, are heated by natural hot springs.

🌰 AIN'T NO MOUNTAIN HIGH ENOUGH . . .

The highest point in Pennsylvania is lower than the lowest point in Colorado.

Mount Cook in New Zealand is the largest mountain in Oceana, at 3,764 meters.

The 1968 film *Krakatoa: East of Java* had a major fault. The volcano was, in fact, west of Java.

Australia is the only continent without an active volcano.

HOME ADDRESSES

In Indiana, there is a town named Santa Claus.

The tiniest port in Canada is Port Williams, Nova Scotia.

Desire Street, in New Orleans, runs directly alongside and parallel with Piety Street.

The first European to see New Zealand was Abel Tasman in 1642, but the first to set foot on the island was James Cook in 1769. New Zealand was named after Abel Tasman's home district, Zealand, in the Netherlands.

The official name for Switzerland is the French "Confédération Helvétique"—or the Helvetic Confederation. These initials provide the CH international symbol for Switzerland, which make up car registration plates, stickers, and e-mail addresses.

The town Spa, which gave its name to mineral springs everywhere, is located in Belgium.

Dildo is a town in Newfoundland, Canada.

The oldest town in Belgium is Tongeren.

Grand Rapids, Michigan, was the first city in the United States to put fluoride in its water supply.

Cueta in Spain is actually located in Africa, just across the Straits of Gibraltar.

The capital of Eritrea is Asmara.

The Bronx in New York City is named after the Bronx River. The Bronx River is named after the first European settler in the Bronx—the Scandinavian-born Jonas Bronck, who settled there in 1639.

The city of Mount Vernon, in Washington, claims to produce more tulip blooms annually than Holland.

The only reasonably sized town in the world whose name begins with ABC is the Dutch town of Abcoude.

If Brooklyn, New York, became independent of New York City it would become the third-largest city in the United States after the rest of New York City and Los Angeles.

St. Paul, Minnesota, was originally called "Pig's Eye" after a man who ran a saloon there.

Although Ohio is listed as the seventeenth state in the United States, it is technically number forty-seven. Until August 7, 1953, Congress forgot to vote on a resolution to admit Ohio to the Union.

NATIONAL IDENTITY

The national flower of Greenland is the willow herb.

The floral emblem of Western Australia is the Mangles' kangaroo paw.

The Dominican Republic, Mexico, Zambia, Kiribati, Fiji, and Egypt all have birds on their flags.

Cyprus has a map on its flag.

NATION NOTES

Twenty-eight percent of Africa is wilderness.

Thirty-eight percent of North America is wilderness.

If you told someone he was "one in a million," you would be saying it to about two thousand of them in China.

Zaire is the world leader in cobalt mining, producing two-thirds of the world's cobalt supply.

Only five nations in Europe touch just one other: Portugal, Denmark, San Marino, Vatican City, and Monaco.

There are now said to be more Samoans in Los Angeles than in American Samoa.

Tasmania has the cleanest air in the inhabited world.

Hong Kong has the world's largest double-decker tram fleet.

New Zealand is the only country that contains every type of climate in the world.

Between 1947 and 1959, forty-two nuclear devices were detonated in the Marshall Islands, in the northwest Pacific.

Singapore is the only country with only one train station.

Jamaica's main export is bauxite, which is used to make aluminum.

The country with the biggest percentage of female heads of household is Botswana.

ROAD WORK

The roads on the island of Guam are made of coral. This is because the ground coral sand of the beaches is used to mix concrete instead of importing regular sand from thousands of miles away.

The longest highway in America is Route 6, which starts at Cape Cod in Massachusetts and goes through fourteen states before ending in Bishop, California.

The original cobblestones that were used to pave the streets in New York City were originally weighting stones put in the hulls of ships to keep an even keel.

Woodward Avenue in Detroit, Michigan, carries the designation M-1 because it was the first paved road anywhere in the world.

The London Underground station St. John's Wood is the only station on the network that does not contain any of the letters of the word *mackerel*.

PICKY EATERS

Some Malaysians protect their babies from disease by bathing them in beer.

The inhabitants of Darwin, Australia, drink a yearly average of sixty-two gallons of beer each.

To eat in the Eiffel Tower restaurant you now have to go to New Orleans in Louisiana, where the dismantled restaurant from the famous Paris landmark was reassembled and reopened for business in 1986.

There is a Historical Museum of Spaghetti in Pontedassio, Italy.

LOCAL CURRENCY

The English gold coin, the guinea, is named after the country in West Africa where the gold used to make it was originally mined.

Giraffe tails, woodpecker scalps, and porpoise teeth have all been used as money, somewhere in the world.

Australian five, ten, twenty, fifty, and one hundred dollar notes are made of plastic.

LOCAL CUSTOMS

In Italy it is illegal to make coffins out of anything except nutshells or wood.

The oldest surviving parliament is in Iceland. It first met in AD 930 when Viking chieftains met in the open air to argue their differences.

When members of the nature-worshipping Southern Indian tribe Todas greet one another they thumb their noses instead of shaking hands.

The German Bundestag, the Lower House of Parliament, is the world's largest elected legislative body, with 672 members.

Quebec and Newfoundland are the only two Canadian provinces that do not allow personalized license plates on cars.

In Venice, Italy, all gondolas must be painted black unless they belong to a senior official.

Monaco has the biggest per capita ownership of Rolls Royce cars in the world. In the last survey, in the early 1990s, the figure was one for every 65.1 people.

LOCAL WILDLIFE

The only place in the world where alligators and crocodiles coexist is in Florida.

Hawaii has only two snakes: a sea snake that is rarely seen and a blind snake that lives like an earthworm.

Brazoria County in southeast Texas is the only county in the United States inhabited by every kind of poisonous snake found in the United States and Canada.

There are only three types of snake on the island of Tasmania and they are all deadly poisonous.

Alberta, Canada, has been completely free of rats since 1905.

LOCAL WEATHER

A hailstone containing a carp fell in Essen, Germany.

O Come, All Ye Faithful

FAITHFUL FOUNDATIONS

Forty-three percent of Americans regularly attend religious services.

The largest Catholic church in the United States is the Shrine of the Immaculate Conception in Washington, D.C.

The Crystal Cathedral, founded by TV evangelist Robert Schuller, in Garden Grove, California, is longer than a football field and contains more than ten thousand panes of glass.

EVANGELICAL EXTRAS

In February 1964, evangelist Billy Graham broke his life-long rule against watching television on Sunday—to see the Beatles first appearance on American television.

The city with the highest per capita viewing of TV evangelists is Washington, D.C.

POPE-POURRI

Only one Englishman has become Pope in two thousand years. He was Nicholas Breakspear, or Adrian IV, from 1154 to 1159.

On November 29, 2000, Pope John Paul II was made an honorary Harlem Globetrotter.

BIBLICALLY SPEAKING

A Bible published in England in 1632 left out the word *not* in the seventh commandment, making it "Thou shalt commit adultery." It became known as "The Wicked Bible."

Even though the King James Bible was published in 1611, the Pilgrim fathers carried the Geneva Bible with them to America in 1620. The King James Version had not become popular by then.

The first Bible to be published in America was in the language of the Algonquian Indians.

The New Testament was originally written in Greek.

At six cubits and a span, Goliath's height was some-where between nine feet, three inches and eleven feet, nine inches. A cubit is the distance from the el-bow to the end of the middle finger and can vary from seventeen to twenty-two inches. A span is the distance from the extended little fingertip to the end of the thumb and is approximately nine inches.

When W. C. Fields was caught glancing through a Bible, he explained it with, "Looking for loop-holes."

According to the Bible there are twelve pearly gates.

In addition to the animals there were eight people on Noah's ark. Noah; his wife; his sons, Shem, Ham, and Japheth; and their wives. There were three decks on Noah's ark.

The most common name in the Bible is Zechariah. There are thirty-three of them.

The three wise men were called Balthazar, Cas-par, and Melchior.

Delilah had to cut seven tresses of hair from Samson's head to render him powerless.

Salome's dance was the only solo dance mentioned in the Bible.

Some biblical scholars believe that Aramaic did not contain a way of saying "many" and used a term that has come down to us as forty. This means that when the Bible refers to forty days it actually means "many days."

The only domestic animal not mentioned in the Bible is the cat.

There are nine ranks of angels. From the highest to the lowest, they are Seraphims, Cherubims, Thrones, Dominions, Virtues, Powers, Principalities, Archangels, and Angels.

The shortest verse in the Bible is "Jesus wept." (Gospel of John 11:35)

AGING GRACEFULLY

Moses was 120 years old when he died.

The only woman whose age is mentioned in the Bible is Sarah, who bore Abraham a child, Isaac, when she was ninety. She was said to die at the age of 127.

Methuselah lived to be 969 years old, according to Genesis.

JESUS CHRIST, SUPERSTAR

In New Mexico more than eleven thousand people have visited a tortilla chip that has the face of Jesus Christ burned on it.

Jesus is believed to have spoken Aramaic, the language then in use in the Arabian peninsula where he lived. A modern version of the language is still spoken in Syria.

The names of the two thieves crucified with Jesus were Dismas and Gestas.

SPIRITUAL SCOOP

There are 806 million Roman Catholics and 343 million Protestants.

The latest day in the year on which Easter Sunday can fall is April 25. The earliest is March 22.

The term *Xmas* did not originally begin with the Roman letter *X*. It began with the Greek letter *chi*, which was used in medieval manuscripts as an abbreviation for the word *Christ*. For example, *Xus* equals *Christus*.

The film *The Ten Commandments*, in which Charlton Heston plays Moses, was the biggest cinema box-office earner of the 1950s.

Brigham Young, the Mormon leader, married his twenty-seventh, and last, wife in 1868.

The holy cities of Islam are Mecca, Medina, and Jerusalem.

A church council in the twelfth century declared: "A Christian man is bound to chastise his wife moderately."

Preachers who traveled on horseback through the old West were known as "circuit riders."

Sonny and Cher, at the start of their careers, appeared in Bible advertisements produced for the American Bible Society.

DEFUNCT DEITIES

The Vikings had a god of snowshoes named Ull.

The goddess of the rainbow, in Greek mythology, was Iris.

THEY BEG TO DIFFER

Nell Gwynne once quieted an angry Oxford crowd, who mistakenly believed she was Charles II's French Catholic mistress, by telling them: "Pray, good people, be civil. I am the Protestant whore."

Prince Charles once threw the moderator of the Church of Scotland into a fountain at Balmoral.

The American newspaper columnist H. L. Mencken wrote: "Puritanism—The haunting fear that someone, somewhere, may be happy."

The savage Salem witch trials in the seventeenth century were all based on a single line in Exodus: "Thou shalt not suffer a witch to live."

According to Scottish novelist and politician John Buchan, "An atheist is a man who has no invisible means of support."

Lord Hugh Cecil believed "the two dangers which beset the Church of England are good music and bad preaching."

A Sporting Chance

LEARNING THE LINGO

Bowling was originally known in ancient Germany as *Heidenwerfen*, which means "strike down the heathens."

In archery, when an arrow pierces another arrow, which is already in the bull's-eye, it is called a "Robin Hood."

In horse racing, a walkover is when a horse is uncontested in a race and simply has to walk the course to win.

A bad shot that turns out well in golf is known as a "Volkswagen" in golfing slang.

A throw of five on the dice is known as "a Little Phoebe" in craps.

The game of billiards gave us the word *debut*. It is derived from the French word *débuter*, which means "to lead off."

The phrase *turning point* comes from chariot racing. It was the place where a chariot driver turned at each end of the stadium.

The "pone" is the person who sits on the dealer's right in a card game.

Zugzwang is a situation in chess when all possible moves are to a player's disadvantage.

The word *furlong* in horse racing—a distance of an eighth of a mile—dates from the days when a race was a furrow long, the length of a ploughed field.

IN THE RING

Heavyweight boxing champion Ken Norton was rejected for the role of Apollo Creed in the 1976 film *Rocky* because he made star Sylvester Stallone look too small.

Boxing world champion Rocky Marciano nicknamed his deadly right hand "Suzi-Q."

The French boxing federation officially banned fighters from kissing one another at the end of their bouts in 1924.

America's last professional bare-knuckle boxing bout, in 1889, went to seventy-five rounds. The fight was between John I. Sullivan and Jake Kilrain—Kilrain lost. The famous lawman Bat Masterson was the timekeeper.

Professional boxing gloves weigh eight ounces.

All five sons of heavyweight boxing champion George Foreman are named George.

The heaviest heavyweight boxer to compete in a title fight was Italy's Primo Carnera, who weighed 270 pounds when he beat Tommy Loughran in 1934.

OLYMPIC GLORIES

In the original Olympics, trainers were required to attend in the nude. This was to stop women sneaking into the competitions, from which they were banned. One woman had attended an event disguised as her son's trainer. Thereafter the nude ruling was brought in.

The colors blue, red, yellow, black, and green were chosen for the Olympic rings because at least one of them appears on the flag of every nation in the world.

There were no rounds when boxing was introduced at the twenty-third ancient Olympiad in 776 BCE. Contestants fought until one man either dropped or gave in. There were no breaks.

In the ancient Olympic Games, archers used tethered doves as targets.

Oscar Swahn was the oldest person to win an Olympic medal. The Swede won a silver medal for shooting in 1920 when he was seventy-two.

Germany is the country that in 1936 established the modern Olympic tradition of having the flame carried from Greece to the site of the games.

The discus throw is the only track-and-field event for which a world record has never been set in Olympic competition.

Fourteen-year-old Nadia Comaneci of Romania was the first ever to receive a perfect "10" in an Olympic gymnastic competition. That was in 1976.

TEE-D OFF

King James II of Scotland banned golf in 1457 because, he said, it distracted the men from archery practice needed for national defense.

The par for the world's longest golf hole—the 909-yard seventh hole on Japan's Sano golf course—is seven.

The odds against a professional golf player scoring a hole-in-one are fifteen thousand to one.

RUNNING A "RACQUET"

The first tennis millionaire was Australian Rod Laver in 1971. He was twice Wimbledon champion.

When you hit a tennis ball it spends just 4/1000 of a second in contact with the racquet.

Catgut, used in stringing tennis racquets, comes from the intestines of sheep, horses, and several other animals—but definitely not the cat. It is possible the word was shortened from the original *cattlegut*.

The fastest tennis serve ever recorded was that of Bill Tilden, in 1931, which was measured at 163.6 miles per hour.

King George VI competed at Wimbledon in 1926 when he was duke of York. The left-hander lost his first-round doubles match.

The first woman to wear shorts at Wimbledon— on the center court—was Lili de Alvarez in 1931.

The world's fastest racquet sport is badminton, where the shuttlecock reaches speeds of nearly two hundred miles per hour.

HORSEPLAY

Horse racing has a sex allowance. Mares are permitted to carry three to five pounds less weight when running against males in a Thoroughbred horse race.

Horses race clockwise in England and counterclockwise in the United States.

The standard pitching distance in a game of horseshoes is forty feet for men and thirty feet for women. The maximum permitted weight of a shoe in a game of horseshoes is two and a half pounds.

Jockeys are strapped to their mounts with Velcro during camel races in Abu Dhabi.

A rodeo cowboy has to stay on the bull for only eight seconds in a bull-riding contest—but few make it.

IT'S A GAMBLE

The odds of getting four of a kind in a five-card deal in poker are 4,164 to one.

There are over 600 billion possible bridge hands that can be dealt from a pack of cards.

The odds against hitting the jackpot on the average slot machine are 889 to one.

The French dice game known as "Hazard" was introduced into the United States—in New Orleans—in 1813, by a Creole. Creoles, because of their French associations, were sometimes nicknamed Johnny Crapauds, the word *crapaud* being French for toad or frog. At first it was referred to as Crapaud's game, but was later shortened to "Craps."

SPEEDING TO VICTORY

The first man to run the four-minute mile, England's Roger Bannister, held the world-record title for only forty-six days. Australian John Landy knocked 1.4 seconds off his time on June 21, 1954.

The oldest driver in the 1979 Le Mans twenty-four-hour endurance race was actor Paul Newman.

In cross-country bike racing the initials BMX stand for Bicycle Moto Cross (X).

During a hundred-meter race, a top sprinter makes contact with the ground only some forty times.

The first driver to cover a mile in less than a minute in a gas engine car was Barney Oldfield in 1903. He did a mile in 59.6 seconds driving a Ford 999.

The first Indianapolis 500 motor race in 1911 was won at an average speed of 74.59 miles per hour.

FOR LOVE OF THE (VIDEO) GAME

The Japanese company Nintendo made playing cards before it became involved in making computer games.

The very first video game, introduced in 1972, was Pong.

RULES OF ENGAGEMENT

The game of ninepins, taken to America by the Dutch in the seventeenth century, was changed to tenpins in the 1840s. Because of heavy gambling on the game,

New York and Connecticut banned ninepin bowling. But since the ban did not apply to bowling in general, a tenth pin was added to get around the law.

The International Skating Union recognizes forty-eight different types of figure-eights.

The only sport that takes place on a triangular race-course is sailing.

BLOWING THE COMPETITION AWAY

In 1956 the Physical Culture and Sports Commission of communist China recognized the sport of hand-grenade throwing.

Food Fight

HIGH SPIRITS

In America 69 percent of men and 57 percent of women drink beer.

Beer was often served with breakfast in medieval England.

The oldest recipe in existence is a recipe for beer.

Germany has a beer ice cream in Popsicle form. Its alcohol content is lower than that of normal beer.

Manufacturers of Old Grandad whisky produced their product throughout Prohibition by marking the bottles "for medicinal purposes."

The first name of blind cellar monk Dom Perignon, who discovered champagne, was Pierre.

The father of the Gimlet cocktail was Sir T. O. Gimlette, a British naval surgeon who insisted his fellow officers drink gin and lime juice as he believed it to be healthier than drinking neat gin.

The coiffe is the metal wire basket that holds a champagne cork in place.

Queen Victoria mixed her claret with whisky. The resulting brew was her favorite alcoholic drink.

President Kennedy's wife, Jacqueline, had the recipe for daiquiris pinned to the wall of the White House kitchen. It was the couple's favorite drink.

In making bourbon whisky 51 percent of the grain that is used must be corn.

MILKING A SITUATION

In Hong Kong soy milk is as popular as Coca-Cola is in the West.

Cream does not weigh as much as milk.

More people are allergic to cow's milk than to any other food.

Guests to multimillionaire Alfred de Rothschild's mansion in Buckinghamshire, England, who asked for milk in their tea were offered a choice between "Hereford, Jersey, or Shorthorn."

Eighty-seven percent of fully fat milk is water.

THE MUPPET DIET

Miss Piggy once said, "Never eat more than you can lift."

SWEET DELIGHTS

The ancient Romans often paid their taxes in honey.

In Denmark, Danish pastry is known as Vienna bread.

Pound cake received its name from the one-pound quantities of the main ingredients—sugar, butter, eggs, and flour—used in the original recipe.

PIE CHARTING

The largest apple pie ever baked was forty feet by twenty-three feet.

At McDonald's in New Zealand they serve apricot pies instead of cherry ones.

IN THE NUT HOUSE

Pecans are the only food that astronauts do not have to treat and dehydrate when flying in space.

Almonds are members of the peach family.

The peanut is a vegetable and a member of the pea family.

FRUITOPIA

You can make a glass of apple cider with only three apples.

The pineapple originated in South America and did not reach Hawaii until the early nineteenth century.

There are no bananas in banana oil. It is a synthetic compound made with amyl-alcohol and gets its name simply from its banana-like aroma.

The largest fruit crop on earth is grapes—followed by bananas.

FOOD FRENZY

After a coffee seed is planted, it takes five years before the resulting plant can produce consumable fruit.

In order for decaffeinated coffee to be so labeled, under American federal regulations, it must have 97 percent of its caffeine removed.

Butter was the first food product allowed by law to have artificial coloring. It is totally white in its natural state.

In Japan, Christmas Eve is a time to eat strawberry shortcake and fried chicken.

Pepper is the top-selling spice in the world. The second is mustard.

The nutmeg tree produces two spices. Nutmeg is from the nut kernel itself and mace comes from the kernel's lacy covering.

Tabasco sauce is made by fermenting vinegar with hot peppers in a French oak barrel, which has three inches of salt on top and is aged for three years until all the salt is defused through the barrel.

In 1867, Napoleon III commanded chemists to

produce a special kind of food for the army and navy. It was margarine.

Tic Tacs contain carnauba wax—the same ingredient found in many car polishes.

More cat food is bought in Britain each year than can be eaten by the number of cats in the country.

Sarsaparilla is the root that flavors root beer.

A can of Spam is opened every four seconds.

The Pilgrims ate popcorn during the first Thanksgiving dinner.

You cannot taste food unless it is mixed with saliva. This is true for all foods.

French fries were invented in Belgium.

Turnips turn green when sunburned.

Bombay duck is dry, salted fish.

It takes seventy-five thousand crocus flowers to produce one pound of saffron—which is why it is the most expensive spice in the world.

The herring is the most widely eaten fish in the world.

Wild rice is not rice but a coarse annual grass that grows in shallow water or marshland.

Dr. Miles's compound extract of tomato—an early ketchup—was sold as a medicine in the nineteenth century.

Black-eyed peas are beans.

The first commercially manufactured breakfast cereal was shredded wheat, made by Henry Perky in 1882.

Ancient Egyptians would place their right hands on onions when swearing an oath. Its round shape symbolized eternity.

I Wanna Sex You Up

SEXUALLY ACTIVE

A recent survey revealed that 25 percent of Swedish women had had sex with more than fifty men.

Humans spend two years of their lives making love.

Four popes died while participating in sexual acts.

Seventy percent of Swedish women claim to have participated in a threesome.

Every year more than eleven thousand Americans hurt themselves trying out bizarre sexual positions.

The average sexually active woman has sex eighty-three times a year.

The average person spends two weeks of their life kissing.

In a recent survey prostitutes revealed that the sexual act they are most often asked to perform is fellatio.

ENERGY TO BURN

Married women are physically and mentally less healthy than single women.

Sex burns off 360 calories an hour.

A real orgasm is said to burn 112 calories. A fake orgasm is said to burn off 315 calories.

The heart beats faster during a brisk walk or a good argument than it does during sexual intercourse.

Forty-six percent of women say a good night's sleep is better than sex.

TO PROTECT AND SERVE

The Ramses condom is named after the great pharaoh Ramses II, who fathered more than 160 children.

England first introduced sex education in schools in 1889.

More than one million condoms are sold each day in the United States—that being only 0.4 percent of the population.

America's first manufactured condoms appeared in 1870 and were made of vulcanized rubber. They were thick, insensitive, and intended to be reused.

ANATOMY LESSONS

On average it takes two tablespoons of blood to make a man's penis erect.

Elvis Presley called his penis "Little Elvis."

Men are four times more likely to sleep in the nude than women are.

Nudity in public was considered perfectly acceptable in ancient Greece, but it was declared indecent if a man revealed an erection.

Seventy-one percent of women between the ages of eighteen and twenty are at ease being seen nude by their lovers; 51 percent of men are at ease being seen nude by their girlfriends.

The average bra size is now 36C. Ten years ago it was 34B.

The sperm count of American men is down 30 percent from thirty years ago.

VENTURESOME VENUES

Americans spend more money each year at strip clubs than at all the theaters and classical concert halls in the country combined.

One in every three hundred births in the United States occurs in a vehicle.

According to a Caribbean cruise line 58 percent of the passengers are unable to wait more than ten hours before making love. A lifeboat is the fourth most popular place on a ship to have sex. The whirlpool bath is ranked the first.

Placing a red light outside a brothel to advertise its wares was first introduced in 1234 in Avignon, France.

It is against the law to have sex on a parked motorcycle in London.

SELF LOVE

A candle is the artificial device most frequently used by women during masturbation, according to a recent American survey.

Eleven percent of women and 5 percent of men claim never to have masturbated.

In ancient Greece and Rome dildos were made out of animal horn, ivory, gold, silver—or even glass.

LET'S TALK ABOUT SEX

Less than 30 percent of parents say they can openly discuss sex with their children.

Today there is a 75 percent chance that a TV program during family viewing time will contain sexually related talk or behavior.

Only 31 percent of men admit to looking at other women when in the company of their spouse or girlfriend. Their partners say this figure is actually 64 percent.

Sixteen years and two months is the average age for the loss of female virginity in the United States.

Most exhibitionists are married men.

Menstrual cramps have been known, in rare cases, to induce orgasm.

The word *pornography* is from the Greek pornographus, meaning "writing about prostitutes."

In ancient Rome, men found guilty of rape had their testicles crushed between two stones as a punishment.

A winged penis was the city symbol of Pompeii, the ancient Roman resort town destroyed by the eruption of Mount Vesuvius.

Homosexuality was still on the American Psychiatric Association's list of mental illnesses until 1973.

Men experience higher blood pressure during orgasm than women do.

Romans had three words to describe kisses: the kiss for acquaintances, the *basium;* the kiss between close friends, the *osculum;* and the kiss between lovers, the *suavium.*

FRIGID IN MORE WAYS THAN ONE

The average penguin has only one orgasm a year.

STAT SHEETS

WOMENLY FIGURES

Sixty percent of British women believe their legs to be about average.

Thirty percent of British women think their legs are poor.

One percent of British women think their legs are perfect.

Thirty-nine percent of women who think their legs are fat still wear short skirts.

Ninety percent of Irish women are unhappy with their legs.

Forty percent of Scottish women have legs that are different lengths.

Forty percent of women admit to having thrown footwear at men.

In 75 percent of American households, the women manage the money and pay the bills.

MANLY ASSETS

Ten percent of men do not care what their partners' legs look like.

Eighty-three percent of people hit by lightning are men.

Eighty-five percent of men do not use the front opening of their underpants when they urinate.

Six percent of American men say they proposed to their wives on the phone.

INTERNATIONAL NUMBERS

Twelve percent of the British population is left-handed.

Ninety-seven percent of Canadians wouldn't borrow a toothbrush if they forgot to pack their own.

About thirty thousand Americans are injured by toilets every year.

Half of all Americans live within fifty miles of where they grew up.

There is a lawsuit every thirty seconds in the United States.

If the population of China began walking past you in single file, the line would never end because of the rate of reproduction.

LAW OF AVERAGES

The average number of alcoholic drinks consumed by male marathon runners in a week is fourteen.

The average person laughs thirteen times a day.

The average person has more than 1,460 dreams a year.

The average person over fifty will have spent a year looking for lost or mislaid items.

The average human produces fifty thousand pints of spit in a lifetime—the equivalent of two small swimming pools.

The average person in America spends eight years of his life watching television.

Right-handed people live, on average, nine years longer than left-handed people.

On average, each year 55,700 people are injured by jewelry.

The average iceberg weighs twenty million tons.

A four-year-old child asks an average of 437 questions a day.

In a lifetime the average person spends eighteen months on the telephone.

'TIS THE SEASON

Forty-eight percent of people say that Santa Claus and gift-giving detract from the religious celebration of Christmas.

Forty-four percent of people say they spend too much at Christmas.

Twenty-two percent of men leave their Christmas shopping until the last two days before Christmas Day. Only 9 percent of women do the same.

Twelve percent of people start their Christmas shopping with the January sales.

ANIMAL ANSWERS

Sixty-seven percent of dog owners buy holiday gifts for their pet.

Seventy-eight percent of pets never travel with their owners.

Forty-five percent of cat owners buy a holiday gift for their pet.

Ninety percent of bird species are monogamous.

If you had enough water to fill one million goldfish bowls you could fill an entire stadium.

LAST WORDS

"This is no time to be making new enemies."
   —Voltaire, in reply to the bishop of Paris when asked on
      his deathbed to renounce the devil and turn to God

"The earth is suffocating. Swear to make them cut me
open, so I won't be buried alive."
   —Frederic Chopin

"I'm sorry to disappoint the vultures."
   —Stephen Ward, Profumo-scandal scapegoat

"I've had eighteen straight whiskies—I think that's a
record. After thirty-nine years this is all I've done."
   —Dylan Thomas

"Tell me, Gene, is it true you're the illegitimate son
of Buffalo Bill Cody?"
   —Actor John Barrymore, speaking to a deathbed friend

"I realize that patriotism is not enough. I must have no hatred or bitterness toward anyone."

—Edith Cavell, the British nurse executed as a spy

"If I say good night to you now, will you promise that I won't wake up again?"

—Film producer Alexander Korda

"I think I could eat one of Bellamy's veal pies."

—Prime Minister Pitt the Younger

"Dammit. Put them back on. This is funny."

—Gunfighter "Doc" Holliday, after his boots were removed

"You can do that more easily to my dead body. Come, be quick!"

—Louis Philippe, duke of Orleans, speaking to the executioner removing his boots

"The bullet hasn't been made that can kill me."

—Gangster "Legs" Diamond

"Get my 'swan' costume ready."

—Russian ballerina Anna Pavlova

"Drink to me."

—Pablo Picasso

"I can't sleep."

    —*Peter Pan* author James Barrie

"It would really be more than the English could stand if another century began and I were still alive. I am dying as I have lived—beyond my means."

    —Oscar Wilde

"Be natural, my children. For the writer that is natural has fulfilled all the rules of art."

    —Charles Dickens

"Take away those pillows—I shall need them no more."

    —Lewis Carroll

"What is the noise?"

    Daughter: "It's the people outside."

    "What are they doing?"

    Daughter: "They've come to say 'Good-bye.' "

    "Why? Where are they going?"

    —Dictator Generalissimo Franco

"Nothing but death."

    —Jane Austen, when asked if she wanted anything

"Death, the only immortal, who treats us all alike, whose peace and whose refuge are for all. The soiled and the pure, the rich and the poor, the loved and the unloved."

—Mark Twain

"If I feel in good form I shall take the difficult way up. If I do not, I shall take the easy way up. I shall join you in an hour."

—King Alfred I of Belgium, killed mountain climbing

"Prithee, let me feel the axe. I fear it is not sharp enough. Do not hack me as you did my Lord Russell."

—James, Duke of Monmouth, beheaded

"Oh God, here I go!"

—Heavyweight boxer Max Baer

"Can this last long?"

—King William III

"In the name of modesty, cover my bosom."

—Elizabeth, sister of King Louis XVI, guillotined

"I am always angry when I'm dying."

—Clifford Mortimer, barrister father of John

"Good night, my darlings, I'll see you tomorrow."

—Noel Coward

"I've never felt better."

—Actor Douglas Fairbanks Sr.

"Do you know where the apothecary lives? Then send and let him know that I would like to see him. I don't feel quite well and I will lie still until he comes."

—Duke of Wellington

"Sister, you're trying to keep me alive as an old curiosity. But I'm done. I am finished. I'm going to die."

—George Bernard Shaw

"Well, I've played everything but a harp."

—Lionel Barrymore

"I desire to go to hell and not to heaven. In the former place I will enjoy the company of popes, kings, and princes, while in the latter only beggars, monks, and apostles."

—Niccolò Machiavelli

"That was the best ice-cream soda I ever tasted."

—Comedian Lou Costello

"See that Yul [Brynner] gets star billing. He has earned it."

—Gertrude Lawrence, star of the film *The King and I*

"If you would send for a doctor I will see him now."
—Emily Brontë

"Now I want to go home. Don't weep. What I have done is best for all of us. No use. I shall never get rid of this depression."
—Vincent van Gogh

"I guess you were right, Wyatt. I can't see a damn thing."
—Police officer Morgan Earp, speaking to his brother, Wyatt, who denied afterlife existed

"I should never have switched from scotch to martinis."
—Humphrey Bogart

"This is it. I'm going. I'm going."
—Al Jolson, Russian-born American singer, film actor, and comedian

"I'm going. Perhaps it is for the best."
—President John Tyler

"This is my final word. It is time for me to become an apprentice once more. I have not settled in which direction. But somewhere. Sometime. Soon."
—Lord Beaverbrook, British Conservative politician and newspaper proprietor

"There is no one in the kingdom that will make me his master. My time has come to die."

—Confucius

"On the whole, I would rather be in Philadelphia."

—W. C. Fields

"I do not know which is more difficult in a Christian life—to live well or to die well."

—Daniel Defoe

"May I please have a cigar?"

—John Ford, film director

"I think it's time for morphine."

—D. H. Lawrence

"Please put out the light."

—President Theodore Roosevelt

"The executioner is, I believe, an expert and my neck is very slender. Oh God, have pity on my soul."

—Anne Boleyn

"I can't feel anything in my right leg. I can't feel anything in my left leg. Doctor, are my eyes open? I can't see."

—"Manolete," matador

"I always was beautiful."
>—Pauline Bonaparte, Napoleon's sister

"What is the scaffold? A short-cut to heaven."
>—Charles Peace, hanged killer

"I have offended God and mankind because my work did not reach the quality it should have."
>—Leonardo da Vinci

"Excuse my dust."
>—Dorothy Parker, wit

"Now I know that I must be very ill, as you have been sent for."
>—Henry Longfellow

"My fun days are over."
>—James Dean

"Remember me to my friends. Tell them I'm a hell of a mess."
>—H. L. Mencken, journalist

"What matter how the head lie, so the heart be right? 'Tis a sharp remedy, but a sure one for all ills."
>—Sir Walter Raleigh, when told his head lay the wrong way for beheading

"A king should die standing up."
> —Louis XVIII of France, trying to rise

"That was a great game of golf."
> —Bing Crosby

"Go away. I'm all right."
> —H. G. Wells

"God bless. Goddamn!"
> —James Thurber

"Better not. She would only ask me to take a message to Albert."
> —Prime Minister Benjamin Disraeli, asked if he wished
> to see Queen Victoria at his deathbed

"Don't let it end like this. Tell them I said something."
> —Mexican revolutionary Pancho Villa

"If this is dying, then I don't think much of it."
> —Lytton Strachey, English author

END QUOTES

"Death is the most convenient time to tax rich people."
—Prime Minister David Lloyd George

"Once you're dead, you're made for life."
—Jimi Hendrix

"Either he's dead or my watch has stopped."
—Groucho Marx

"He makes a very nice corpse, and becomes his coffin prodigiously."
—Oliver Goldsmith, Irish novelist, poet, essayist, and dramatist

"It's not that I'm afraid to die. I just don't want to be there when it happens."
—Woody Allen